What Others Say About *They Serve Like We Lead*

A great customer service strategy starts on the inside with your employees. This book is a must read for every leader in customer service.

Shep Hyken, New York Times bestselling author
of *The Amazement Revolution*

They Serve Like We Lead is a must-read for any leader looking to improve their effectiveness as a leader while inspiring the best in their team. Monique has structured the book in a way that inspires both learning and action. Her superb and accessible writing style makes this both an entertaining and impactful read. Being fortunate enough to know Monique as well as I do, I know that this book is a true reflection of how Monique shows up every day in her own life. You will be thankful to have this book in your arsenal.

Christine Churchill Burke, Founder & CEO,
Customer Service Institute of America

They Serve Like We Lead is not merely an informative book on how to engage, empower and develop your organisation, leaders and team.

Monique's anecdotal writing style embraces humour, incredible knowledge, underpinned by her undeniable love and compassion for all people. Her genuine value of people makes this an outstanding book as it ensures the reader reflects on the importance of validation, care and support for employees. Monique has humanised a leadership book.

Ernie Merrick OAM, Chief Football Officer,
Football Australia

Monique Richardson has put together what I consider to be mandatory reading for any leader in the customer service industry. Monique takes you by the hand and guides you through how to be a strong service leader –

from understanding what service leadership is, to implementing it within your business and most importantly why you need to do so. The chapter summaries are thought-provoking and profound. I am incredibly inspired to commit to the list of actions I have made to ensure that I can be the best version of myself and to serve our teams so they can serve our customers.

Cassandra Byrne, Customer Experience Manager,
Hickinbotham Group

I recently had the pleasure of reading *They Serve Like We Lead* and I have to say, it's a great read. Monique's writing style is engaging and filled with humour and real-world experience, making it a joy to read. But what really sets this book apart is Monique's deep love and compassion for people, which shines through on every page.

As someone who has worked in leadership roles for many years, I found Monique's insights and strategies to be incredibly valuable. The tips and opportunities for reflection give the reader time to think and put into practice in real time. But what really resonated with me was her emphasis on the importance of care and support for employees. In today's fast-paced business world, it's easy to forget that our people are our most valuable asset. Monique's book is a powerful reminder of that fact.

Overall, I can't recommend the book enough. It's a must-read for anyone who wants to build a strong, engaged and empowered team, and who truly values the people they work with.

Matt Baker, General Manager Member
& Customer Experience, Venues NSW

From the moment I met Monique, I knew she would inspire me and my team; she has a presence and warmth that is infectious, and you cannot fail to be energised by her professionalism and passion for service leadership. As I read this book after a tough week at work, I could hear her voice narrating it and I found myself smiling as I felt encouraged and compelled to be a better service leader. I cannot agree more that employee engagement and customer experience are intrinsically linked.

The book is packed with fabulous thought-provoking quotes and the chapter summaries provide practical tips and an opportunity for self-reflection that will resonate at all levels of an organisation. I know I will be sharing this book with my workplace and a well-thumbed copy will have pride of place on my desk ready for those moments when I need a motivation boost. However, what I love most about this book is the sentiment that jumps from every page, Monique truly uses her life experience and relationships to shape her service vision and does so with elegance, empathy and humility.

If you are embarking on an organisational culture change or want to move the dial from good to great this book is a must read. Grab yourself a cuppa and immerse yourself in a leadership journey that will really make the difference.

Rachel Spencer, Managing Director,
Transdev John Holland Buses (NSW)

Monique, thank you so much for the opportunity to read your book *They Serve Like We Lead*. You truly have crafted a guiding tool that unlocks many critical key fundamentals to allow aspiring leaders really to understand and learn how to become inspirational, effective leaders of people and teams. Doing so will deliver you so much satisfaction as a manager of teams, son or daughter, or parent.

Leadership is hard; it's tough and rewarding and will challenge you in ways you never imagined. It revolves around people and being genuinely invested in others — their interests and their career paths and the effort required to develop people to deliver outcomes beyond their capabilities or skill sets that come naturally.

In this book you have explored and brought to life the learnable skills that will allow any aspiring career driven individual become a service leader who delivers outstanding results. I wish I'd had a book like this in my own leadership journey. It would have had a tremendous impact knowing it's okay to make mistakes and okay to try new ways to achieve results whilst always ensuring that my priorities are people and their development.

I highly recommend this book for all leaders, regardless of experience or their career phase. It will challenge you and reinforce the power of passion, dedication and investment in others. These will pay you back tenfold with results and most importantly the gratification that your teams are achieving outcomes that only others could imagine.

Donovan Stevens, Vice President & General
Manager Institutional / FRS ANZ, Ecolab

They Serve Like We Lead is a must-read for any business leader who wants to take their customer service to the next level. It's a comprehensive guide that provides a clear roadmap for building a customer service culture rooted in the principles of leadership and employee engagement. It's a game-changer because it emphasises the importance of taking care of your people first, in order to create an environment where they can exceed customer expectations.

I especially appreciated Monique's understanding of the importance of leading by example. The book provides numerous examples of companies that have successfully created a customer service culture by putting their employees first and empowering them to make a difference. The stories are both inspiring and instructive and demonstrate the power of servant leadership in action.

This book is for anyone who is serious about creating a customer service culture that is both sustainable and impactful. Monique's insights and strategies are practical, actionable, and grounded in real-world experience. I highly recommend this book for those who want to take their customer service to the next level.

Amanda Gray, Manager Customer Service Strategy & Operations,
Training Quality and Regulation, NSW Department of Education

Great customer service cannot happen if organisations write cheques their employees can't cash. Agile, insightful, and wide-ranging, Monique Richardson's book offers a constructive synthesis between customer first and employee-first proponents. At a time when many organisations view their workforce as a cost centre, *They Serve Like We Lead* makes a compelling case that happy employees lead to happy customers, and in turn, business success. This is important reading.

Merlin Kong, Innovation & Digital
Transformation, Kiah

The connection between CX and EX is more powerful now than ever. In this book, Monique expertly takes the reader on a journey combining her knowledge and experience with her genuine desire to serve others as she shares logical strategies and how to introduce these to any organisation looking to make impactful change. Imagine a world where all leaders adopt just some of her practical tips and the kind of WOW experience we could create for our people, ourselves and the communities we serve.

Janine Hill, General Manager Customer Experience
& Markets, Wilson Security

They Serve Like We Lead should be a staple in every leader's toolkit. The framework, principles and values Monique explores in this book should be the mainstay of every leader's philosophy.

It is clear that Monique has both lived experience and passion in an extensive career built upon helping businesses and individuals to improve their service leadership style and practices. As Monique demonstrates with her insightful and entertaining scenarios, this has a profound ripple effect on a business' bottom line and the global and local customer communities we serve.

Monique has well and truly inserted a well-needed dose of empathy and compassion into her approach that has direct evidence-backed links to company and people performance.

In this post-Covid world where the way we work and connect is rapidly changing, this book could not be more timely in helping businesses and individuals adopt and grow competitively and in a socially sustainable way. It will no doubt inspire and attract our future forward thinking service leader generations.

I'm so impacted by the learnings and practical anecdotes of this book that I will certainly keep a hard copy at my desk as a beacon to guide my leadership roles.

Sue Emery-Smith, Senior Manager
Professional Services

I have been inspired by Monique's passion for people for many years. When I learnt that she had written a book on service leadership I was very excited to get my eyes on a copy as I just knew it would be a fantastic read, and boy was I right!

They Serve Like We Lead takes a deep dive into service leadership providing real life examples and emphasizes the importance of understanding people with a focus on empathy and compassion and how this approach leads to better business results and a more fulfilling work environment.

The book is an excellent resource for any leader looking to improve their skills and make a positive impact within their organisation. Monique's passion for people and service shines through on every page, making this book a must-read for anyone interested in service leadership.

Angela Koya, Customer Experience Coordinator,
Moorabool Shire Council

What a great read! So many 'Argh' and 'Yep' moments where the book resonated with me completely and refreshed content we can so easily forget. The power of bringing research into this space and linking it to suggested activities and reflective questions makes this book a great tool for leaders working through this content with their teams. It provides a great framework to break down service leadership into many core areas and develop internal workshops around these topics. I am so glad I got the chance to read this book and I have pages of notes to follow up and action within our business. Loved it!

Kate Klein, General Manager People &
Corporate Services, Clublinks

Monique is a brilliant service leadership expert who has delivered training in our organisation. Her new book includes her well-constructed framework. It's full of real-world examples, stories and practical tips. *They Serve Like We Lead* is an entertaining and informative must read for any leader in service industry.

Morgan Ryan, Chief of Clinic Operations
– SA, TAS & WA, Capitol Health

They Serve Like We Lead

They
Serve
Like We
Lead

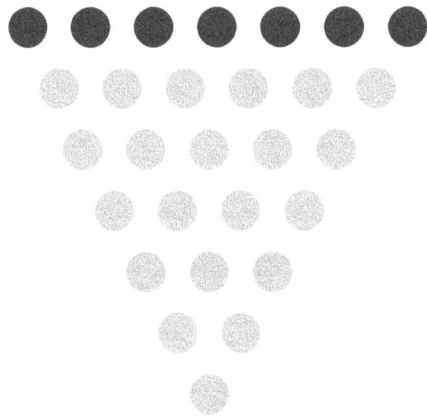

How to take
care of your people
so they take
care of your customers

MONIQUE RICHARDSON

Published by Monique Richardson.

First published in 2023 in Melbourne, Australia.

Copyright © Monique Richardson

www.moniquerichardson.com.au

The moral rights of the author have been asserted.

Edited by Jenny Magee.

Typeset and printed in Australia by BookPOD.

ISBN: 978-0-6457927-0-6 (paperback)

ISBN: 978-0-6457927-1-3 (ebook)

NATIONAL LIBRARY OF AUSTRALIA

A catalogue record for this book is available from the National Library of Australia

Acknowledgements

So many people make a difference and have an impact when you write a book.

First and foremost, my heartfelt gratitude to my family; my incredible husband Scott and our four amazing children, Molly, Jai, Kobi, Lucy, and my beautiful Mum. Your continued support, encouragement and cheering keep me inspired and motivated. You are my absolute world and the reason behind everything I do. I love you with all my heart.

I would also like to acknowledge and thank Matt Church, Lisa O'Neill and Col Fink. You are living, breathing examples of service leadership, care and community. To the entire Thought Leaders Business School community, thank you for the constant inspiration and the joy you bring to my life. Joining Thought Leaders has transformed my life in the most extraordinary way possible. I have never met a more caring, thoughtful, humble and inspiring group of people.

To my exceptional editor, Jenny Magee, I am forever grateful for the gift of you in my life. Your patience and faith in me and my book have helped and inspired me beyond words. Working with you again on my second book has been a true privilege. Thank you for always believing in me and my work.

To my mentors, Colin Ellis and Jane Anderson. Colin, thank you for your belief and example and for helping me to create my vision and take action. I continue to learn so much from you about commitment, dedication, excellence and delivering value. Thank you, Jane, for your ongoing support and inspiration. You have taught me so much about building a practice based on heart, love and care. Thank you for always being there. Your generosity truly knows no bounds.

Thank you to my dear friends and accountability tribe: Sophie Kranz, Mark Butler, Katie Rees and Shane Williams. There is truly nothing better than a group of friends who support, challenge and make you laugh until you cry. It is my honour to walk alongside you.

A special mention to Alex Hagan, Emma McQueen, Mary Butler and Paul Matthews, whose words and faith in me have made such a difference. Thank you for your check-ins and advice and for being there when I needed you most.

To my extended family and friends who have continued to encourage and support my work, I feel so blessed to be surrounded by such incredible souls who continue to enrich my life.

To my wonderful executive assistant, Irina Pacheco, you have been a constant source of support over the past couple of years, and I am blessed to have you in my world. Thank you for your care for our clients and me.

My thanks to Sylvie Blair from BookPOD for all your support in publishing my second book, Popy Aker for your exceptional graphic design skills in bringing my models to life and Taofeek Abdul Qoyum for the book cover design.

To Miss Catherine Judd, my Year 12 teacher. You changed the course of my life with your belief in me, and I am forever grateful. I know I would have never written this book if not for you.

And finally, to every service leader and team member in our customer service community who has inspired this book. Every connection, conversation and workshop has meant the world to me. I learn so much from you. Seeing the impact of your work and the difference you make every day in the lives of your team and customers is truly inspiring.

In loving memory of my late father, Noel Francis Richardson, for teaching me everything I ever learned about how to be of service to others and the power of the legacy we leave behind.

Contents

Part Four: Embed

Part Five: Culture

Foreword

When Monique Richardson asked me to write the foreword for this fabulous book, I was somewhat surprised and incredibly honoured. So much so that I began to think that surely someone else was more qualified than me to do this (and would likely do a better job!). I called Monique to ask that exact question and she assured me she wanted me to do it. Now I have the challenging job of trying to put into words why this book is such a fantastic resource for anyone who wants to be a better leader.

I am the general manager of Venue and Event Services at the Melbourne Cricket Club. We are a private club with over 150,000 members, responsible for managing the Melbourne Cricket Ground (MCG), the eleventh-largest stadium in the world. We have approximately seventy major events each year and welcome more than 3.5 million people through the gates annually. In 2022, we were the third most attended venue in the world.

I first met Monique in early 2016 as we looked to revolutionise our customer experience at the MCG. We looked at off-the-shelf training programs but ultimately decided to develop a bespoke customer service program called CARE, which was rolled out to all of our staff and contractors. To date, more than 8,000 people have been involved in the CARE program. Not only did Monique assist in developing the program, but she has also personally facilitated more than 150 face-to-face training sessions with our staff and contractors.

Since then, our CARE program has won several customer service awards, including first place at the Australian Service Excellence Awards for a large business in 2019 and first place at the International Service Excellence Awards for a medium business the following year. Our customer experience scores are consistently higher than 8/10, and Monique has been integral to the program's success.

My first impression of Monique was someone whose passion for customer service shone through from the moment we met. She is warm, engaging, an exceptional listener and goes out of her way to ensure that people are comfortable around her. As soon as I saw her facilitate the first training session with our casual staff, I knew we had hit the jackpot. She is a brilliant facilitator who has that rare ability to engage with a wide range of people without having to try. She does it with ease and lives and breathes the themes in this book.

Service leadership is more than being a good leader; it is about being a good person. This book explores service leadership in detail and provides simple, practical, easily implemented service solutions for leaders at any level. It is full of straightforward examples of leaders from many industries who bring unique perspectives to what success looks like.

At the MCG, our research indicates that the average patron has six touchpoints or interactions with our staff when they visit. In 2022, that was 21 million opportunities to either enhance someone's experience or ensure it is memorable for all the wrong reasons. Through Monique's skills and experience, we have developed a culture that emphasises people — both customers and visitors — and gives us the best opportunity to provide exceptional service in every interaction with every customer at every event.

I thoroughly enjoyed this book, and I am sure you will too. I hope it motivates, inspires and empowers you to become the best service leader you can be. I hope you find the concepts, ideas, practical tips and reflection questions as valuable as I have, and I wish you well on your service leadership journey.

Josh Eltringham
General manager Venue and Event Services
Melbourne Cricket Club

Preface

'There are many things in life that will catch your eye, but only a few that will catch your heart. Pursue those.'

– Michael Nolan

I fell in love with customer service at the age of fourteen years and nine months. I was working at a supermarket delicatessen and loved interacting with my team and customers. I got to know customers well, some by name, some by their order, and quickly realised the power of customer service and connection and how it could impact another human being.

After working in various customer service and training and development roles, including my last role as a national training manager for a Fortune Global 500 Company, I started my practice in the year 2000. My dear friend, Peter Pangalo, advised me to specialise in what I was most passionate about, which, of course, was customer service. Since then, I have worked with many wonderful clients delivering frontline customer service training programs.

After yet another session of listening to the challenges a team was experiencing with a less-than-ideal leader, it hit me like a bolt of lightning. It didn't matter what I did in frontline training; if the leadership didn't enable their people to deliver exceptional service experience, all other efforts would fail.

So began my passion for service leadership. At the heart of this work is my underlying philosophy: Take care of your people so they can take care of the customer.

The title of this book is inspired by John Sainsbury, the founder of the UK supermarket chain Sainsbury's, who said, 'They serve like we lead'. That line summed up everything I had ever seen and heard working with frontline teams and the impact of leadership on a team's ability to deliver world-class experiences to its customers.

As a keynote speaker and trainer, I have had the privilege of working with more than 50,000 customer service professionals and leaders across the globe. They have inspired this book. Across twenty-two years of research, observation and experience working with many businesses and industries across several countries, I have no doubt that service leadership makes the greatest difference to the team member and customer experience.

We all have customers, whether external or internal. I love the simple definition of customer service as 'taking care of the people we serve'. The strongest service cultures have an organisation-wide commitment to taking care of their customers, whether in frontline or support roles that serve those who directly serve customers.

What makes the difference in service-driven organisations? A service leader who drives a strong service culture regardless of the customer or department.

Service leadership transcends all industries. Over the years, I have worked in commercial, government and not-for-profit sectors in every industry imaginable. These have included events, healthcare, local government, sport and recreation, banking and finance, telecommunications, insurance, logistics, universities, retail and luxury retail, automotive, and real estate. I tailor each engagement to the organisation and the outcomes may be different. However, the underlying service leadership principles outlined in these books apply to any people leader in any industry.

Caring for your team is at the heart of all service leadership.

Throughout this book, I use the terms service leadership and service leaders. My work is built on the work and shoulders of giants in the field of servant leadership, including Robert Greenleaf, Ken Blanchard, Max De Pree and many others. My approach stems from the underpinning philosophies of servant leadership and aligns with the premise that the core role of the leader is to serve first and to be of service to their team.

Leadership is the lever that drives customer focus. It is also the most significant enabler of any team member's ability to deliver an exceptional service experience. The level of customer focus of a team is directly proportionate to the leader's focus. It begins with the CEO and the executive and extends to every people leader within the organisation.

We are at a time when competition for talent remains fierce, and an organisation's ability to attract and retain people has become a leadership imperative. Organisations must provide an exceptional employee experience across all touchpoints, from recruitment and onboarding to career development. With remote work becoming mainstream, work-life balance (61%) is top of mind, according to Gallup. In addition, companies with a strong purpose are an attractive proposition, especially to millennials and Gen-Z.[1]

Service leadership and caring for people matter now more than ever.

Introduction

'Our great collective calling in the world today is to enhance joy. That takes leaders with great hearts and great courage who seek only to serve, to imagine a better future and to devise ways in which we can realize it together.'

– Dr Raj Sisodia

The world needs strong service leadership. Recent years have been tumultuous and significantly impacted organisations across the globe. How we work has changed; the new normal of hybrid and remote workplaces has changed how we lead. Impacts such as the Great Resignation have highlighted the importance of nurturing and caring for people. With so much change and disruption, the role of a service leader is critical.

How you lead and care for your team will directly affect employee engagement and customer experience.

I've written this book in five parts.

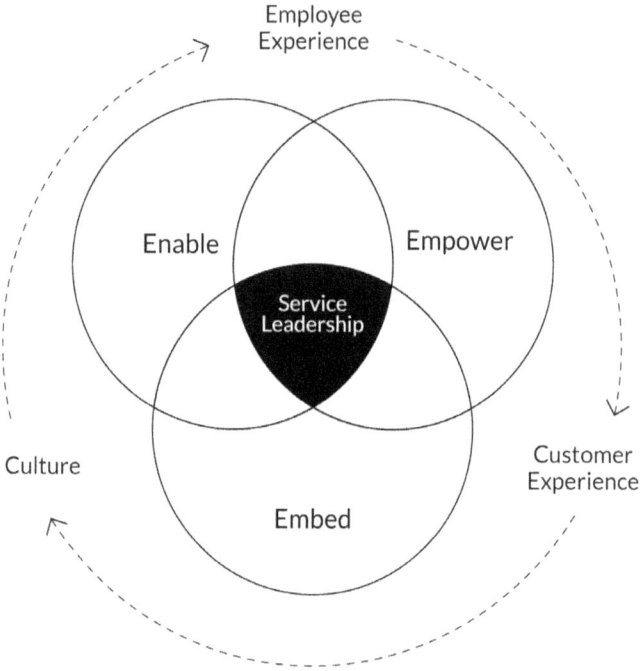

Figure 1: Service Leadership Model

Part One: Leadership

Service leadership is the underpinning foundation of this entire book. Any leader in any organisation will ultimately impact the level of customer focus of the team. How well you lead your team and how much you care about each team member will be reflected in how well your team takes care of the customer. Happy customers are the result of building a happy team.

Part Two: Enable

In service leadership, the leader must enable their people to deliver a superior customer experience. No one turns up to work to deliver poor customer service or do a bad job. There is a strong link between the customer and the employee experience. The employee experience is integral in enabling people — from recruitment and selection to orientation and onboarding. Enabling is about setting the team up for success and giving people everything they need, from standards, tools and training to technology.

Part Three: Empower

A service leader empowers their team through knowledge, decision-making and discretionary spend. The more a leader can empower their team, the better the experience for everyone, including customers, team members and leaders. Decisions are made quickly, customers are not kept waiting, and team members feel more pride and satisfaction. The foundation of empowerment is trust. When team members feel trusted, they are empowered to act in the best interests of the customer and the organisation.

Part Four: Embed

The role of a service leader is to embed the service-driven behaviours they wish to see through coaching, feedback, recognition and accountability. Customer service is not a stand-alone training program or a one-off event. The service leader's role is to keep customer service alive. It must be their key focus. Every. Single. Day.

Part Five: Culture

Service leadership is the primary driver for creating a customer-focused culture and establishing a culture of care. That includes care of self, care for each other and care for the community. Organisations and leaders that genuinely care for their people and extend that care into the community through being more socially conscious, impact employees, their customers and the wider world.

Just like my training programs, this book is designed to be practical. It is a *doing* book. American author Napoleon Hill wrote that knowledge is not power; it is potential power. It is what we do with knowledge that counts. My work focuses on taking action and creating results.

So, grab your highlighter, pencil or pen and make notes in the margins. Each chapter ends with a summary, reflection questions and actions to take. You will find your final action plan at the end of the book. Use this for the next twelve months and focus on implementing the ideas you have generated.

I hope this book inspires you to reflect on your current successes, identify opportunities and take action to put the knowledge to work.

PART ONE

LEADERSHIP

Chapter One

Servant vs Service Leadership

*'Servant leadership is a philosophy
and set of practices that enriches
the lives of individuals, builds better
organizations and ultimately creates
a more just and caring world.'*

– Robert K. Greenleaf

Servant leadership is a timeless concept that has been around for decades. It is a leadership philosophy in which the leader's goal is to serve first. Robert K. Greenleaf is regarded as the founder of modern-day servant leadership. He coined the term in his 1970 essay, *The Servant as Leader*.[1] Servant leadership turns the old hierarchical model of leadership completely on its head.

Yet servant leadership is an old concept; two thousand years ago, it was central to the philosophy of Jesus. Renowned servant leaders have included Dr Martin Luther King, Nelson Mandela, Mother Teresa, Mahatma Gandhi, and modern-day CEOs such as Max De Pree. In servant leadership, the leader's primary responsibility is to provide service to others. Taking care of other people's needs is the highest priority. It is always about putting other people first.

Servant leadership is characterised by humility, as this leader recognises they have much to learn from those they lead. Servant leaders are not motivated by position or power, but rather by caring for others.

The world has seen the impact of self-serving leaders whose focus is command, control and power. Leading from traditional positional leadership is more centred around hierarchy, the bottom line and an obsession with outcomes, often at the expense of people. This damages trust and creates an environment where business outcomes are more important than people.

Have you ever worked with a leader whose leadership style was autocratic? What was your experience? It is perplexing that there are still leaders who lead through power and fear when we have access to so much literature and evidence of the positive impact of humane and caring leadership philosophies and disciplines. The results of this leadership style show in low engagement surveys, high attrition rates, absenteeism and negative customer sentiment. If you treat your people poorly, this will show up in how they treat your customers.

Understanding the terminology

Servant leadership is not to be confused with servitude. Nor is it about sacrificing your own needs, wants and desires for others or working yourself into the ground. It is not about being a slave to your team or taking over their responsibilities. At all times, it is choosing to do the right thing. It is entirely possible to put the needs of your people first without sacrificing your own needs.

As author Dan Cable wrote in the Harvard Business Review, 'Humility and servant leadership do not imply that leaders have low self-esteem, or take on an attitude of servility. Instead, servant leadership emphasizes that the responsibility of a leader is to increase the ownership, autonomy and responsibility of followers — to encourage them to think for themselves and try out their own ideas'.[2]

When used out of context or if you're unfamiliar with the work of Robert K. Greenleaf and others, the word 'servant' could pose an issue for how we respond to this concept of leadership. In some cultures, the word is offensive, conjuring negative connotations and stigmatising in the corporate world. There is documented history of servants being subjugated and mistreated.

In early historical definitions, a servant was defined as a male or female personal or domestic attendant, one owing duty of service to a master or lord, one employed by another and subject to his orders. The word came from the old French 'servant', or foot-soldier, and the verb 'servir', meaning to attend or wait upon.

While the word 'servant' is rarely used today, exploring the term in leadership and its meaning in a modern context is essential.

Comprehensive research and application of the principles of servant leadership have profoundly impacted the lives of those who lead and those being led, as well as organisational culture and the bottom line. Many companies named in Fortune's annual listing of the *100 Best Companies to Work For* espouse servant leadership and have integrated it into their corporate cultures.[3]

Organisations that practise servant leadership include Zappos, Nordstrom, Whole Foods Market, Marriot International and Starbucks. All are legendary for delivering world-class customer experiences. Research from Emlyon Business School in France indicates that servant leadership improves employee morale and increases company profit.[4] This research confirms that servant leadership is good for people management and employee morale and positively impacts company performance and profitability.

Characteristics of a servant leader

Larry C. Spears extracted ten essential characteristics of a servant leader from the writings of Robert K. Greenleaf.[5] Spears viewed these as central to the development of servant leaders. The ten traits comprise the following:

Listening

Leaders have always been admired for their ability to communicate and make decisions. Although the servant leader must have these abilities, they must be strengthened by a strong commitment to listening closely to what others say. The servant leader works to identify the group's will and aids in its clarification. They pay careful attention to both spoken and unspoken messages. Hearing one's inner voice is included in the process of listening. The servant leader's growth and wellbeing depend on listening and times of reflection.

Empathy

The servant leader tries to comprehend and feel what others are going through. People must be accepted and celebrated for their distinctive spirits and exceptional qualities. Even when refusing to accept particular actions or performances, they assume good intent on the part of coworkers and colleagues and do not reject them. The most effective servant leaders have developed their listening skills to include empathy.

Healing

Relationship healing is a potent catalyst for change and integration. Mending relationships with themselves and others is one of servant leadership's leading advantages. Many people are emotionally wounded, and while this is a characteristic of being human, servant leaders recognise that they can contribute to healing others. If the idea that the pursuit of wholeness is something they share is implicit in the covenant between the servant-leader and the led, then something subtle is transmitted.

Awareness

The servant-leader is strengthened through awareness in general and self-awareness in particular. We can better grasp moral, political and ethical issues by becoming more aware of them. It makes viewing a more comprehensive, integrated approach to most problems easier. Awareness doesn't bring comfort; it brings clarity and wakes people up. Effective leaders are typically alert and disturbed. They do not look for solace but are at peace within themselves.

Persuasion

Another quality of servant leaders is that they rely on persuasion rather than positional power when making decisions. Instead of imposing their will on others, a servant leader tries to persuade them. This is where the traditional authoritarian approach and servant leadership are most obviously different. The servant leader is skilled at fostering group consensus, emphasising persuasion over coercion.

Conceptualisation

Servant leaders can think outside the box to approach an issue or organisation from a new perspective. This trait necessitates discipline and practice for many leaders. The need to meet immediate operational goals consumes the typical leader. Servant leaders must broaden their thinking to include more expansive conceptual thinking. They strike a careful balance between intellectual thought and a practical approach to day-to-day operations.

Foresight

The capacity to predict the most likely conclusion of a situation is difficult to describe but simpler to identify. It is closely tied to conceptualisation and enables foresight. A valuable trait of a servant leader is the foresight to see the consequences of decisions, lessons learned from the past, and the reality of the present. It has a strong foundation in the intuitive mind.

Stewardship

Peter Block has defined stewardship as 'holding something in trust for another'. According to Greenleaf, all institutions should be held in trust for the view of society, and CEOs, team members and trustees have important roles to play. Like stewardship, servant leadership assumes a commitment to meeting the needs of others. Additionally, it places more emphasis on the use of openness and persuasion than on control.

Commitment to people's growth

The servant leader is dedicated to the personal growth of every team member. They are aware of their immense responsibility to exert every power to foster professional and personal growth. In practice, this can entail (but is not limited to) specific acts, such as providing finances for professional and personal growth, showing genuine interest in people's opinions, encouraging employee participation in decision-making and actively supporting those made redundant to find new jobs.

Building community

The servant leader feels that much has been lost in recent human history as the major impact on people's lives has shifted from small groups to large institutions. Because of this awareness, the servant leader seeks strategies to encourage a sense of belonging among employees of a given organisation.

According to servant leadership, a true community can be developed among those who work in organisations like businesses and other institutions.

Service leadership builds on servant leadership

As indicated earlier, I use the terms 'service leader' and 'service leadership'. This idea draws heavily on the philosophies of servant leadership and acknowledges those who have contributed to this important field of work.

My focus is not a new leadership theory; instead, it is the practical application of the principles of servant leadership. It is about leading in a way that demonstrates care for people, ultimately impacting the customer.

I believe that leaders are there to serve their people and be of service to others. Service leadership enables you to lead in a way that engages your people and your customers. That includes your team, your own leaders, coworkers, and other departments and even extends to your suppliers and partners. The ripple effect of this is enormous. The more you care for your people, the more they will care for your customers and provide them with a better experience, ultimately making for a happier and more caring society.

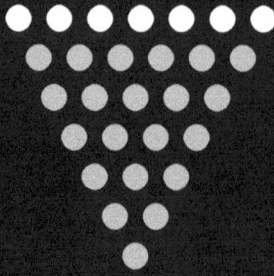

Chapter Summary

Practical tips

- At the start of the day, create an intention to 'serve' rather than 'lead' your team.

- Examine your leadership style. How is it aligned with the principles of servant leadership?

- Consider the ten characteristics of servant leaders. Which are your greatest strengths? Where could you focus more?

Reflection questions

- What is your reaction to the term 'servant leadership'?

- What is your leadership intent? Is it to serve yourself or serve others?

- Who are the servant leaders that you know and admire? What qualities do you see in them?

Actions to take:

Chapter Two

The Role of a Service Leader

'Example is not the main thing of influencing others. It is the only thing.'

– Albert Schweitzer

The true role of a service leader is deeply caring for people. It focuses on serving first and leading second. Never underestimate the importance of service leadership on the individual, the team, the organisation and the customer. It is how the service leader chooses to lead and show up each day. It is having a humble and caring heart and wanting to make a difference in the lives of others.

As Max De Pree wrote in *Leadership Is An Art*, it is 'liberating people to do what is required of them in the most effective and humane way possible'.[6] Service leaders listen to their people and act on their feedback. They coach and mentor their teams and enable individuals to reach their full potential. They lead people where they need to go and develop future leaders. They focus on the whole person realising that when we are at work, we bring our whole selves. True service leaders get to know their team members as individuals. They know their strengths, opportunities, what is important to them and their needs and preferences.

Top traits of exceptional service leaders

Across more than two decades of work, I've recognised the following traits in service leaders that their people value deeply.

They engage the team in the vision and the purpose

Service leaders have a way of connecting the team with the organisation's vision and purpose. They ensure each team member knows the importance of their role and how they fit into the big picture. This is very powerful in creating a service culture, as each person needs to see why what they do matters.

I recall a conversation with an exceptional people leader in a cleaning chemical business. In a hospital lift, he had chatted with a cleaner about their work. The cleaner said, 'I'm not important. I am just a PSA (Patient Services Attendant).' The leader replied, 'You have one of the most important roles in this hospital. Your work saves lives.' In that moment, he helped the team member see the purpose of their work and the bigger picture of their role in infection control. He made them feel important.

One of my personal service leader heroes is the late Tony Hsieh, founder and CEO of online shoe retailer Zappos. The company is famous for its employee and customer experience. Its mission is 'Delivering happiness'. Zappos has ten core values that help achieve its purpose, one of which is 'Deliver WOW through service'. The leaders live and breathe the organisation's purpose. It is the focus of recruitment, onboarding and induction and is part of the company's DNA. Zappos was sold to Amazon in 2009 in a deal worth around

US$1.2 billion, proving that you can take care of your people and customers and still be highly profitable and successful.

They spend time with customers on the frontline

Great service leaders get in and get their hands dirty. Richard Branson of Virgin Atlantic is known to jump behind the counter and serve customers. He regularly travels on flights asking customers for feedback and taking notes for future action. True service leaders happily serve customers on the frontline when it is busy or just make it part of their monthly plan to ensure they are visible and close to the customer and the team.

In one organisation I worked with, the CEO and directors spent time taking customer calls in the contact centre. During his time as CEO of Telstra, David Thodey AO was known for calling customers regarding their complaints. This action built rapport and connection with customers and had a powerful impact on the team. In his words, 'leaders need to be seen talking to and about customers, asking questions, listening to their stories, making a difference. Real change comes from real actions.'

Gail Kelly was the first female CEO of Westpac, one of Australia's big four banks. An incredibly successful leader, she led a cultural transformation by putting people and customers at the heart of the organisation. After a brief career in teaching, Gail began in customer service as a bank teller and loved the engagement of a customer-facing role. This passion continued throughout her career. As CEO, maintaining engagement with customers and people was a core priority. She had a rigorous schedule that included making calls to customers each Friday and a full day every quarter, where she went out to branches to spend time with customers and team members.

They empower the team to make decisions

Teams need to feel trusted to know they can help in the moment without reverting to unnecessary rules and processes. They must feel empowered through decision-making and discretionary spending to help the customer without needing to refer to their leader, while knowing they can always ask the leader for support. Even when a team member seeks advice, a service leader uses this as a coaching opportunity and asks, 'What would you like to do for the customer?' using an empowering question as a teaching moment rather than telling.

They remember people's names and details

From the CEO to the team leader, frontline people consistently mention this as a standout attribute. While it is easy to remember your team members' names, it makes a massive impact when the leader remembers everyone's name, their children or pets, and even where they were going on holiday. Such conversations profoundly impact how a team feels about a leader. At the end of the day, we all walk around with an invisible sign on our heads that reads 'Make me feel important'. The little things count, and exceptional service leaders show genuine care and interest in people and create meaningful connections in their everyday interactions.

They are fair and consistent

Fairness is often raised by team members when describing exceptional service leaders. This is highlighted by leaders who appreciate differences yet apply standards consistently. They gain respect from the team by being clear in their expectations and not showing favouritism. They are open and transparent. Everyone knows where they stand, which generates high trust in the leader and builds team morale.

They recognise freely and easily

Successful service leaders have an abundance mindset regarding recognition and have developed this as a daily leadership habit. They make use of opportunities to recognise individuals and the team. They sincerely and genuinely thank their team at the end of each day and focus on formal and informal recognition.

Gratitude is the foundation of a service leadership mindset. Service leaders continually look for ways to show care and appreciation. Celebrating people shows how much you value them.

They ask for feedback from the team and take action

One of the most powerful attributes of a service leader is regularly asking the team for feedback, ideas and opinions and then listening to that feedback and taking action. Many of the best ideas for improvement come from the frontline. I refer to this as the 'goldmine of frontline feedback'. Frontline team members are closest to the customer and often bring brilliant ideas for improving the customer experience. They hear customer pain points, challenges and struggles and have suggestions for making the customer experience easier and more positive.

This goes beyond the annual engagement survey; it must include giving people a formal and informal outlet to continually raise problems and ideas. Service leaders have a regular cadence of checking in with the team to obtain their feedback and work to close the feedback loop.

The leader has the team's back

One of the most important things for a team member is to feel that the leader has their back. Even if a decision is not in line with what the team member has advised the customer, the leader will explain why they have done so. People always give their best when this attribute is evident and it is integral in creating a high-trust environment.

They protect their people at all times and will not tolerate customer abuse

A critical responsibility of every leader is to ensure the protection, safety and wellbeing of team members. This includes having clear policies and procedures to safeguard the team, with training, coaching and support to equip them to deal with challenging customer situations. A service leader makes themselves available for escalations and supports the team member when a customer displays unacceptable conduct. A customer's behaviour may mean they are asked to leave the premises, a call is terminated or, in serious cases, they are restricted from accessing the business.

I worked with a prestige car dealership whose dealer principal banned a customer from entering their premises; such was the level of abuse they had directed at the receptionist. It is the right of every team member to feel safe at work, and the service leader must ensure they are protected at all times.

Growing levels of customer aggression bring increased organisational and leadership responsibility for the safety and wellbeing of all team members. Clear boundaries must be established, including implementing and socialising the organisation's unacceptable customer conduct policy and clear escalation paths. Training is also a leadership priority, ensuring team members have the skills to diffuse and de-escalate difficult and aggressive behaviour with immediate post-incident support.

They hold the team to high standards

Exceptional service leaders demand excellence. They expect very high personal standards of themselves and others and hold the team accountable to the customer. From the team member's perspective, this is positive and motivates them to achieve results. The leader is very clear about the standards the team must meet. They are there to support, mentor and coach the team to help each individual and the team to meet their goals. In his book *Excellence Wins*, Horst Schulze, the founder of the Ritz-Carlton, wrote of his first teacher, 'He didn't only inspire us; he also held us to high standards'.[7]

Accountability can be done humanely. It is not about driving people into the ground with unrealistic expectations. It is creating a culture of excellence and an expectation that the team delivers a high standard of service for every customer. Every day.

They focus on team strengths

I always remember a conversation with the founder and owner of a successful real estate agency group during a customer service awards presentation I was judging. He shared that the sales agents didn't do any administration. In his words, they were terrible with paperwork and generally had low levels of attention to detail. Yet their strengths were their relationships with customers and their ability to sell. He had set up the working environment so that each agent had strong administrative support. This led to happier team members and happier customers. The seamless workflow and high levels of responsiveness due to job design ultimately increased sales, customer satisfaction and referrals.

The VIA Institute on Character and Gallup have researched strength-based approaches in the workplace based on Martin Seligman's work with positive psychology. In one study, Gallup found that employees feel more confident, self-aware and productive when focusing on strengths rather than weaknesses. This leads to higher employee engagement, increased performance and significantly lower attrition rates.[8] Service leaders shift from a weakness-focused mindset to a strength-based approach with their team and each individual.

They eliminate top-down language

Language is critically important in service leadership. In conversations with leaders, I sometimes hear, 'We need to focus on customer service from the top down or the bottom up'. For me, that's like fingernails across a blackboard. It may seem like a small thing, but language dramatically impacts those who hear it. The language of 'top down' or 'bottom up' leadership is outdated, counterproductive and disempowering. Exceptional service leaders don't use the terms such as the 'people beneath me' or refer to their team as 'subordinates'.

It is disingenuous to describe customer service professionals as being at the bottom of the organisation while simultaneously saying they are cared about and important.

They invert the traditional pyramid

One of my first full-time roles was working as a customer service representative in the Optus contact centre. It was when they first entered the marketplace as Telstra's main competitor. I vividly remember attending the initial interview, where they drew the inverted pyramid on the whiteboard and explained the importance of customers and the frontline. I sat at the back of the room thinking that while it looked fine in theory, my experience in other workplaces meant I shrugged it off as an interesting marketing and PR exercise.

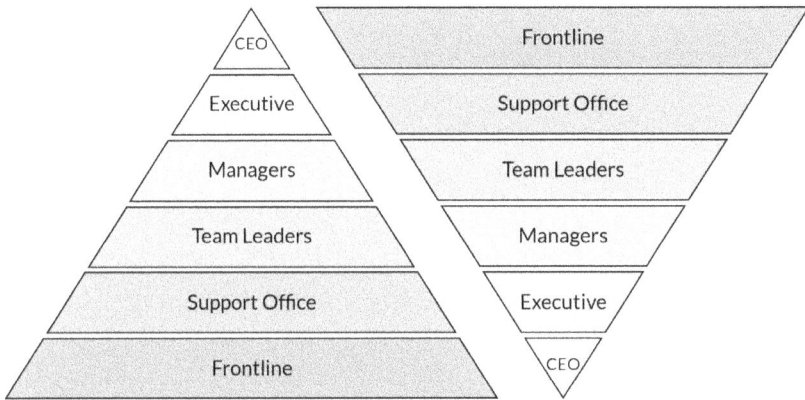

Figure 2: The upside down pyramid

It wasn't until I had secured the role and started working with Optus that I saw their incredible focus on the team and the customer. It began as soon as I was hired and continued throughout my orientation and training.

The way the organisation and the leaders valued the frontline team was reflected in how we were treated, our pay and our benefits. We were cared about and supported, and the leaders maintained an unrelenting focus on the customer experience. They lived and breathed the inverted pyramid model in their words and actions.

If you have access to an organisational chart, it's an interesting exercise to turn it upside down. Notice who is at the bottom — the people who talk to your customers. By flipping it, the CEO and the leadership serve those who serve the customers. In the words of leadership legend Ken Blanchard, 'How can you serve your customers with excellence when your people are serving the CEO?'[9]

They lead with empathy and compassion

Emotional intelligence and levels of self-awareness are characteristics of exceptional service leaders. While empathy has always been a crucial leadership trait, with the many challenges facing individuals, teams and businesses today, it is taking on a new level of importance.

Many teams are doing it tough, with team member shortages, increasingly impatient customers, delays and pressures and challenging demands. The world needs empathetic leaders more than ever.

The best service leaders I have met and worked with have all had high levels of emotional intelligence and the ability to demonstrate empathy for their team and customers. It makes a critical difference to team member engagement. A study by Catalyst revealed that 76% of people who experienced empathy from their leaders reported they were engaged, compared with only 32% who experienced less empathy.[10]

Compassion is another essential attribute. While the words empathy and compassion are often used interchangeably, empathy is an emotion felt for and with others, whereas compassion goes beyond emotion to include the active intention to help others. 'Compassion occurs when we take a step away from empathy and ask ourselves what we can do to support the person.'[11] Leaders who demonstrate both empathy and compassion create much stronger connections and trust with team members.

They lead by example

Great service leaders lead by example. One of the most powerful examples of service leadership in action I have ever witnessed was during a training workshop for the Melbourne Cricket Club (MCC) — ground managers of the Melbourne Cricket Ground (MCG). While the training extended to everyone in frontline and support roles, we commenced the project exactly where all customer service transformation projects need to start — with the leadership team.

Stephen Gough (CEO of the MCC from 1999-2017) attended one of the early workshops to welcome the group and stay for part of the session. As he sat, he noticed a couple of customers who looked lost. Without a word, Gough jumped out of his seat, took them where they needed to go and quietly returned to the training room. In that moment, nothing was more powerful than the example he had just shown. While we explored the theme of service leadership, his actions spoke louder than anything I could have said.

This was the same leader who remembered people's names and conversations and made everyone feel important. He was universally loved and admired because of his genuine care and connection with his people and customers. When things were busy and there were problems or issues, he served with his frontline people at the entry gate. Stephen Gough is one of the most inspiring and humble leaders I've ever met.

The best service leaders lead by actions, not words. The saying 'It's not what you say, it's what you do that counts' is never more critical than when leading customer teams and aiming to build a service-driven culture.

They genuinely care about their people and their customers

Caring deeply for the team and customers is an essential trait in every service leader.

One of my first jobs in retail was working for a beauty products company. Lucy Lewis was a much-loved leader in the business. She was very hands-on, often visiting and spending time in all the stores. We looked forward to her visits — not only for how she interacted and engaged with us but for what we learnt from watching her with customers. Lucy had a way of engaging customers that was so genuine and authentic. She always made them laugh with her wonderful sense of humour.

Soon after I started work with the business, I became seriously ill and spent three weeks in hospital. You can imagine my surprise and joy when Lucy visited me with a gift. I still remember it as an act of care and kindness all these years later.

Service leaders have care at the core of their being. Leaders who take care of their people so they can take care of the customer will always get the best results. Kind, caring, empathetic and inspiring leaders create an environment where their teams will thrive. There is a strong feeling of mutual trust and respect.

In the words of servant leadership expert Ken Blanchard: 'The most effective leaders I know are just good human beings, they care about people. They listen more than they talk. They want to help people win. That's about caring and it's about your heart.'[12]

Caring leaders create long-term success by improving employees' wellbeing, teamwork, engagement and overall organisational performance. It is the role of every service leader to communicate how much they care about their people through their words and actions.

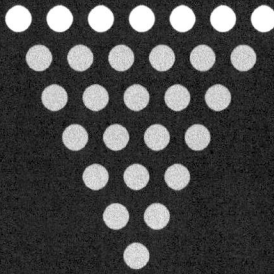

Chapter Summary

Practical tips

- List three leadership traits that are your primary strengths and three that you can develop further.

- Schedule time each month to be with customers and your team on the frontline. Block out the time in your calendar and stick to it.

- Confirm that your team is clear about the service you expect them to deliver.

- Ensure your organisation has a clear, documented and socialised unacceptable customer conduct policy and that the team is fully aware of it.

- Provide the team with training on managing angry and aggressive customers.

Reflection questions

- Do you spend enough time on the frontline with customers and your team? If not, how will you make this happen?

- How much do you focus on your team members' strengths rather than their weaknesses?

- Which leadership traits would make the greatest difference to your team if you focused on them more?

- How do you show your team that you care in words and actions?

- Do you consistently hold your team to high standards of excellence?

Actions to take:

Chapter Three

Who is My Customer?

'Customer service is an attitude, not a department.'

– Tony Hsieh

Service leaders must ensure everyone in the team knows who their customer is. While this may seem obvious, it is not always the case. A few years ago, I was chatting to a participant before a workshop commenced when he said, 'I don't even know why I am here. I don't have any customers.' Surprisingly, I have heard this sentiment expressed more than once!

The foundation of building cultures of service excellence is ensuring everyone in the organisation understands who their customers are. Swedish businessman Jan Carlzon wrote one of my favourite books, *Moments of Truth*.[13] He says, 'If you're not serving the customer, your job is to be serving someone who is'. Customer service is everyone's responsibility. The service leader's role is to ensure everyone in the team understands who their customers are and how they impact the overall customer experience.

Too often, customer service is seen as the responsibility of the customer service department. Nothing could be further from the truth. This type of thinking is dangerous and results in low levels of responsiveness and a lack of ownership and accountability for the customer experience across the organisation. I have repeatedly seen the impact of a team that does not consciously think about its customers and their experience. Consequences include poor customer performance, departmental silos, customers handballed around the organisation, and increased complaints. It can even lead to the loss of customers.

Think about the last time you flew on an aeroplane; perhaps it was on holiday or for business. It wasn't just the frontline team, the pilot and the cabin crew who impacted your experience. It was the baggage handlers, the cleaning team, the catering crew, air traffic control, rostering and scheduling team and even finance and accounts payable. While we are often unaware of it, an entire team effort contributes to our customer experience. That is where the on-stage and off-stage elements of customer service come into play and where each person and department can make a difference. The leader's role is to create this link and help the team see the broader impact of their work.

There are numerous benefits for leaders who ensure their teams know who their customers are. It helps to build stronger customer service cultures, people see how they fit into the big picture, teamwork, collaboration and customer satisfaction levels increase, and re-work and complaints reduce.

It is vital to define customers and increase understanding of customers among all employees. While everyone has customers, the customers each team serves are different. Some teams serve both external and internal customers, while others only serve internal ones. Teams that also work closely with suppliers and partners recognise their importance in delivering an exceptional service experience to customers.

External customers

An external customer is the people or organisations who purchase goods and/or services from us, or are users of a service in a commercial, government or not-for-profit organisation.

Internal customers

Internal customers are those we provide service to within our organisations. These can include our teams, people in other departments, coworkers and our leaders.

Heskett, Jones, Loveman, Sasser and Schlesinger wrote the following in their 2008 Harvard Business Review article, *Putting the Harvard Service Profit Chain To Work*. 'It is particularly difficult for employees to identify their customers when those customers are internal to the company. These employees often do not know what impact their work has on other departments. Identifying internal customers requires mapping and communicating characteristics of workflow, organizing periodic cross-departmental meetings between 'customers' and 'servers', and recognizing good internal service performance.'[14]

I have always maintained that all excellent service starts at home. How we respect and treat each other internally ultimately flows to the customer.

Partners

Many organisations engage suppliers/partners to deliver part of their customer experience. While, by definition, these are not internal or external customers, the relationship must be carefully considered, given its potential impact. I prefer the term 'partner' as it focuses on a partnership approach — working together to deliver the customer experience.

Consider when you purchase goods online. As the customer, you don't care who is responsible for delivering the goods; you just want them to arrive on time. The selection of partners is an integral part of the customer experience. The best of the best show a level of care for their partners. They ensure they align with partners who are equally focused on the customer experience and can deliver their brand promise. Some of the most customer-focused organisations I work with provide customer service training to their partners, such is the recognition of their role in supporting superior customer experience.

If everyone within an organisation has a clear understanding and focus on who their customers are and what they need and expect, a culture of service excellence begins to emerge. This assists in building ownership, pride and accountability. Organisations, departments and individual team members need to consider the following:

- Who are our customers? (external and internal)
- What do our customers need and expect from us?
- How do they currently feel about the service we are providing?
- What are we doing well?
- What could we be doing even better?

Engaging regularly with customers enables you to understand them more deeply. A collective and clear understanding of who your customers are is the first step in creating an organisation-wide responsibility for the customer experience. Every team member has a role in the customer journey, even if they don't have a direct customer service-facing role. It is up to each leader to create the link and align and focus the team. Exceptional customer experiences happen when every leader and every team member in every department across the company are aligned and share the same customer service strategy and vision.

Chapter Summary

Practical tips

- Ensure your team understands who their customers are internally and externally.

- Select partners who are customer-focused and can deliver on your promises.

- Spend time buddying with team members, listening to calls or going out on the road with your internal customers to understand their needs.

- Arrange to meet with your internal customers. Ask them how you could better serve them.

- Organise internal customer satisfaction surveys to see how well you are serving your internal customers. These can be in person or online and conducted every six to twelve months.

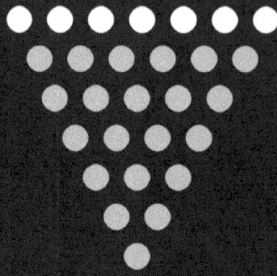

Reflection questions

- Are you confident your team knows who your internal and external customers are?

- Have you spent time with your team helping to create the link between their role and how they impact the customer experience?

- What is your relationship like with your suppliers/partners? Are they customer-focused? Do they represent your brand and organisation? Have you been transparent with your suppliers/partners on your expectation of service delivery?

- How well do you take care of your partners? Do they feel like a valued extension of your team and organisation?

Actions to take:

PART TWO
ENABLE

Chapter Four

The Link Between Employee Experience and Customer Experience

'Over the years, organisations have shifted focus from putting customers at the centre, then employees, and swinging back and forth between the two. But if recent times have taught us anything, it's that the two are intrinsically linked, and one cannot exist without the other.'

– Mark Buckley

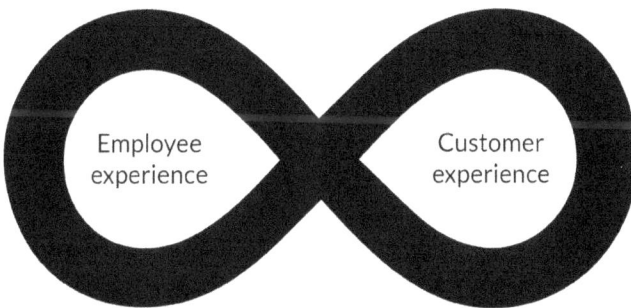

Figure 3: The link between employee and customer experience

There is a critical link between the employee experience (EX) and the customer experience (CX). Key touchpoints determine the employee experience throughout the journey, influencing employee engagement.

Let's define the terms used throughout this section.

The **customer experience** is how customers interact with and feel about an organisation.

The **employee experience** is how employees interact with and feel about the organisation they work for.

The **employee journey** describes the length of time an employee spends with a specific organisation, including all the touchpoints.

Employee engagement is the degree to which employees are mentally and emotionally committed to their work, team and employer.

Who is more important?

Poor employee engagement worldwide has been estimated to cost around US$7 trillion in lost productivity.[1] The level of engagement is determined mainly by the employee experience.

It has been interesting to note the debate between organisations and leaders about who is more important — employees or customers. Some assert that employees should always come before customers. Sir Richard Branson famously said, 'Put your staff first, customer second and shareholders third'. The thinking behind this is that if you take care of your people and they are happy, they will deliver great experiences, which will flow on to abundant shareholder returns.

Yet this position has been challenged by those who believe customers are the most important people in the business. Mantras such as 'The customer is the most important person on our premises' and 'Customers always come first' have permeated many workplaces.

Organisations or teams that put their employees first at the customers' expense can create negative experiences for the customer. I once worked with a very frustrated team who shared that an internal team-building event was scheduled as a priority over a new customer installation. The business subsequently lost the account, which was significant. It's a prime example of internal priorities impacting the customer.

Putting customers ahead of employees can negatively impact the experience of team members who may feel disengaged and even leave. A simple example of this is an organisation that makes promises to a customer that are impossible to deliver and creates enormous stress for employees. Or they might take on a customer project that is impossible to deliver, so team members have to work weekends and evenings, impacting their lives inside and outside of work.

So, which focus is right?

I believe you cannot have one without the other and that customer experience and employee experience are inextricably linked. Everyone benefits when they have concurrent attention — the employee, the customer and the organisation. Employee and customer experience have never been more aligned. Each is vital to the organisation's success; if one area is lacking, the other will ultimately suffer.

With employee talent and retention top of mind in our changing world, improving the employee experience and aligning it to customer experience must be a critical priority for every organisation in every sector.

Dissatisfaction is loud

Numerous dissatisfied employees have voiced their unhappiness about workplaces. A mistreated employee can share their experiences online with a click of a button. Websites such as Glassdoor display reviews and ratings from companies across the globe, which potential job seekers can read before applying for a role. A Google search of 'companies who mistreat their employees' shows a staggering eleven million results. A more conscious society will not tolerate employee mistreatment or a lack of inclusive practices. Customers will act with their feet which will not only impact the organisation but have a massive impact on attracting and retaining talent.

Great employee experiences lead to great customer experiences. The best workplaces are those that care for employees and customers. The hospitality company Marriott International has a long-standing tradition of 'doing whatever it takes to take care of the customer'. It executes this tradition through a strong focus on its employees, whom it refers to as 'associates'. This deeply held belief remains the keystone of the company's culture and is summarised in the words of its founder, J. Willard Marriott. 'If you take care of the associates, they'll take good care of the customers, and the customers will keep coming back.'

The disciplines of employee experience and customer experience can learn much from each other. Employees and customers both desire seamless, connected, personalised and convenient experiences. We want a well-designed and defined end-to-end journey and seek experiences that make our lives easier.

Reducing effort and ease of customer and employee experience is a key differentiator. Both require up-to-date technology that supports their experience and makes it easier to engage with the organisation. Employees and customers are looking for solutions and problems to be solved. They need support and a feedback loop to respond and be listened to. And importantly, employees and customers desire positive emotions that drive loyalty and retention.

So much of the employee and customer experience is about how we make people feel. The service leader must think consciously about how they want their people and team to feel at the end of each day. Author Dr Henry Cloud summed it up beautifully when he said, 'Servant leaders...spend a lot of the time asking themselves that very question about the people they lead: Where are they? Where are my people today — inside their hearts, minds and souls? How does it feel for them to be here? How does it feel to be under my leadership? How does it feel to be on my team or in my department or organization?'[2]

The driving force

Examining the *employee* experience journey is as critical as reviewing the *customer* experience journey. Employee and customer experience are interconnected and independent, and compelling evidence supports how focusing on both makes a tangible difference to organisations. Denise Lee Yohn wrote in Harvard Business Review that 'Customer experience and employee experience are now two of the driving forces of business. Independently, each function leads to valuable relationships — with customers and employees — but when CX and EX are managed together, they create a unique, sustainable competitive advantage.'[3]

In for-profit organisations, this contributes to increased revenue, and companies with highly engaged workforces (employee experience excellence) are 21% more profitable than those with poor engagement. Companies with quality employee experience outperform Standard & Poor's (S&P) 500 by 122%.[4]

It is in the interests of service leaders to focus on both the customer and employee experience, given the measurement of customer feedback through either net promoter (NPS) or customer satisfaction (CSAT) scores, which are regarded as essential metrics for many service leaders.

This trend will only continue. According to Gartner, by 2024, organisations providing a total experience will outperform competitors by 25% in satisfaction metrics for both CX and EX.[5]

Total experience (TX)

The emergence of total experience (TX) as the new discipline in experiences is worth noting. Total experience is a business strategy that aims to create a better, more holistic experience for everyone who engages with an organisation, including customers, employees, users and partners.

Gartner predicts that by 2026, 60% of large enterprises will use TX to transform their business models to achieve world-class customer and employee advocacy levels.[6]

The Harvard Service Profit Chain

While the disciplines of employee experience and customer experience have continued to gain traction over the years, they are not new. The Service Profit Chain was first proposed in 1994 by Harvard Business School experts James L. Heskett, W. Earl Sasser, and Leonard A. Schlesinger. The theory links employee satisfaction to customer loyalty and profitability, as illustrated in figure 4.[7]

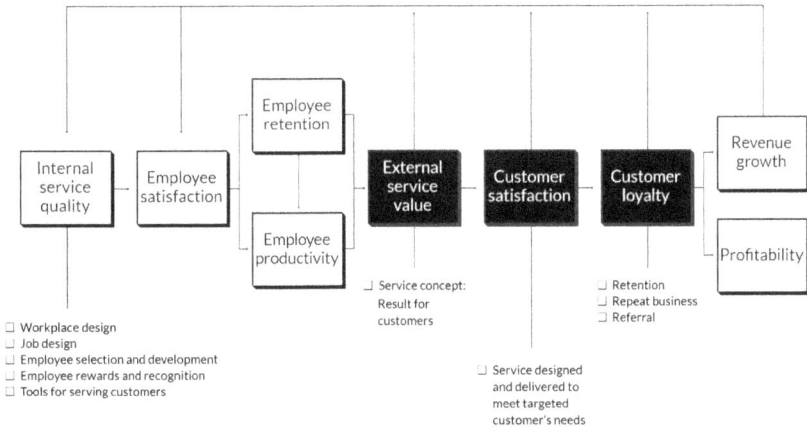

Figure 4: The Harvard Service Profit Chain

The model focuses on the following:

Internal service quality: This is where all service quality begins. Recruiting the right people, providing them with training, recognising their efforts, and ensuring they have the tools and technology to serve the customer. It enables customer satisfaction and customer-focused cultures.

Employee satisfaction: When team members are happy at work and are appropriately supported and motivated, their level of satisfaction and engagement increases.

Productivity: Satisfied, well-trained team members are far more likely to be productive. They have the knowledge, skills and confidence to do their job well and are more willing to go above and beyond for the organisation and its customers.

External service value: Organisations can retain talent and knowledge when the team is happy at work. The team is more productive and satisfied, which inevitably brings more value to the customer.

Customer satisfaction: Customers are ultimately more satisfied when they receive service designed to meet their targeted needs.

Customer loyalty: At the highest levels of customer satisfaction are loyal customers. These are your advocates, your brand ambassadors who will refer you to friends and family, leave positive reviews, and purchase more.

Profit and revenue: At the end of the service-profit chain are profit and revenue. These grow as the number of loyal customers increases.

But where do profit and revenue begin?

It all starts with internal service quality and the employee experience. Ultimately when employees are engaged and highly satisfied, the result is deeper customer connections and an elevated customer experience.

The Service Profit Chain model applies across corporate, not-for-profit and government sectors. While the outcome may differ for each sector, the fundamental principles are identical. Internal service quality drives external service quality. Every service leader is responsible for enabling their team to deliver exceptional customer experiences.

Whether we are customers or employees, our experiences are shaped by interactions and observations. The CEO & co-founder of Yellow.ai, Raghu Ravinutala, says, 'Experiences are ultimately determined by the feelings, emotions and memories accumulated through observation and interaction. The experience usually starts with an interaction that leads to participation, then to engagement, and on to satisfaction, loyalty and advocacy.'[8]

While you can never know how long a team member will stay in an organisation, it is essential to consider how to make each stage both positive and memorable. There is a journey and life cycle for every employee. Each stage represents an opportunity for the service leader to carefully design and craft an experience that makes the team member feel valued, cared about and engaged. Just as you map the customer journey, give the same level of thought and attention to the employee journey.

Mapping your employee journey is an exercise in empathy, helping you understand your current employee experience, along with crucial touch points, pain points and opportunities for improvement.

The employee journey

Lee Cockerell is a former executive vice president of operations for the Walt Disney World Resorts. He believes that no matter how good your products and services are, you can't achieve true excellence unless you attract, develop and keep great people. The employee journey begins with a prospective candidate looking at your job advertisement and continues until the day that employee leaves your company.

We'll unpack the five stages of the journey in Chapters Six through Nine. Figure 5 illustrates the sequence.

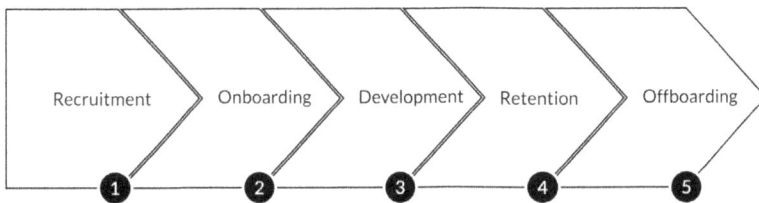

Figure 5: The five stages of the employee journey

Each part of the journey has multiple touch points and must be carefully designed and considered to create a caring, employee-focused, end-to-end journey. The best employee experiences are by design, not by default.

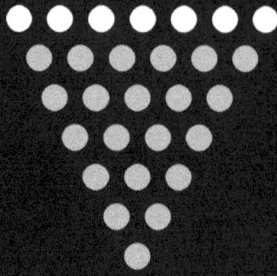

Chapter Summary

Practical tips

- Map your employee journey precisely as you would your customer journey. Write down each stage (use sticky notes) and map it end-to-end.

- Write down the positive elements of the current journey.

- Write down the current pain points.

- Note what you can do to eliminate the pain points at each stage of the employee journey.

- Spend time with a team member who has recently joined the organisation. Ask them to describe the journey and suggest how it could be improved.

Reflection questions

- What is the experience like for your customers?

- What is the experience like for your employees?

- How would you describe your current employee journey?

Actions to take:

Chapter Five

Service Standards

*'All good performance starts
with clear goals.'*

– Ken Blanchard

Building a customer-focused culture starts with identifying and describing what excellent service looks like. That includes clearly defined standards and behaviours for which the organisation wants to be known. They provide clarity for the individual, the team and the leadership by being clear on what the customer wants. They are goals that everyone can work together to achieve.

Aiming to deliver a great customer experience without service standards is like sailing a ship without a compass. They are the true north star of the organisation and a uniting focus for everyone around the customer.

Consider the following table summarising the difference between having service standards and not.

No service standards	Service standards
Unclear expectations	Clear expectations
Difficult to coach or manage performance	Can be used in coaching conversations
Inconsistent service	Consistent service
Poor customer experience	Positive customer experience
Lack of ownership and accountability	Team own the outcomes
Confusion and lack of clarity when starting a role	Useful for orientation and onboarding

Figure 6: How standards make a difference

Service standards define goals and expectations. Without them, customer service is left to individual interpretation, which can vary depending on the person, their background and experience. Standards provide consistency and are unique to each organisation, creating a distinct customer experience.

When I speak with organisations and leaders about raising the capability of their people in customer service skills, the first question I ask is, 'What documented service standards do you have in place?'

You can't count on people to deliver an extraordinary experience if they don't know what is expected of them. It is unfair to the team and the leader.

There are five key steps when incorporating standards into the organisation's culture:

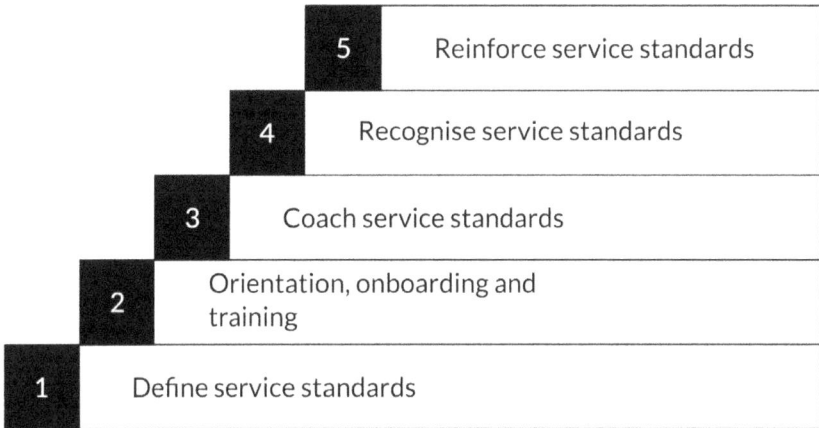

Figure 7: The five key steps of service standards

Define service standards

Standards are benchmarks used to clarify expectations. They should be clear, measurable, observable and realistic. Make them simple, brief, specific and few in number. They must be communicated clearly and continuously and should be attainable.

Behaviours describe how we act or conduct ourselves, especially towards customers. As behaviours are observable, it means they can be recognised and coached.

If an organisation has no service standards in place, I recommend making this a priority. They are an essential foundation for building a service culture. Used in orientation, onboarding, training, coaching and performance goals, they are where all excellent service begins.

Create service standards

How to create service standards

There are many ways to create service standards. The most successful I've seen involve customers, leadership and teams. For maximum impact, I recommend a combination of customer input and feedback and leadership and team input. It is an incredibly engaging process that allows creativity and thoughtful input from a range of stakeholders.

I have generated service standards with events and sports teams, IT and healthcare companies and many others. They apply across every industry. What makes them magical (their special sauce, if you like) is that they are relevant to the customer, the industry and the team and built from within. They are unique to the organisation and its desired customer experience. The most powerful standards are created with team input.

I recently worked with Lounge Lovers, a furniture company that was keen to keep lifting the level of customer service in their delivery team. One of the first steps was working with the team and leaders to develop standards and behaviours they felt would deliver a superior service experience.

The customer experience of purchasing with Lounge Lovers is either in-store or online. However, the organisation recognises the crucial role of delivery drivers in the overall customer journey and experience. Even though they already had very positive customer feedback, they identified an opportunity to take customer experience to the next level.

Rather than simply training the team to deliver outstanding service, the first step was creating service standards for which they wanted to be known. Through an interactive workshop, the team devised a fabulous set of standards and behaviours, and I can honestly say the final result is one of my all-time favourites. They are simple, easy to follow, caring and from the heart. The team were proud and excited to bring these to life.

Engagement in living the standards is always significantly higher when the team has had input. Senior leadership endorsed the standards and the team trained to apply them. They have been socialised throughout the team and will be used in ongoing orientation, onboarding and training. Soon after the standards were introduced, I was thrilled to receive an email from one of the leaders who shared that customer satisfaction was already on the rise.

With permission from Lounge Lovers, I've listed the standards and defined behaviours developed by the delivery team in figure 8.

Our Delivery Team Customer Service Standards & Behaviours

Our Service Standards	Our Service Behaviours
We take pride in our professional presentation	- We are well groomed and wear our clean uniform with pride - We are clean shaven, have clean hands and smell good - We have clean shoes and wipe our boots before entering a customer's home - We maintain a high standard of vehicle presentation inside and out - The customer's home is left in the same state as arrival. All rubbish to be taken when doing assembly. - All packages to be delivered in good condition and presentable when doing a basic drop
We delight our customers and go the extra mile	- We are happy to see our customers and greet them with a smile and use their name - We are eager to go the extra mile wherever possible, for example unpacking for the elderly and recommending after care with products - We anticipate and solve potential issues - We give great tips on easy assembly
We communicate with our customers and keep them informed	- We provide timely communication pre-delivery - We call in advance with a precise eta, also asking for further instruction such as truck parking access and any other difficulties we may encounter - We arrive when we say we will - We are aware of time windows and proactively update the customer if we are going to be outside the window and communicate any delays
We do it once and do it well	- We have high levels of attention to detail and thoroughly check the manifest - We deliver in full and on time and get it right the first time - We deliver to the customer's room of choice
We are knowledgeable and helpful	- We have great product knowledge - We show empathy for the customers' experience to date with earlier delays or other issues - We turn a bad experience into a positive experience

loungelovers

Figure 8: Lounge Lovers' delivery team service standards (included with permission)

Have you ever had a furniture delivery? Was your experience like this? As a life-long fan of interior design, I have never had an experience that reflected the standards and behaviours of the Lounge Lovers' team. If I had, it would be warm and memorable, and I would want to use the company again. I imagine I would also tell my friends and family about the experience. The little things like wiping boots and considering the elderly don't just speak to service; they speak to a deep level of customer care.

There is a visible difference between saying, 'I want you to deliver great service' and giving the team a clear set of standards to work towards. When the team is involved in creating the standards, magic truly does happen.

Make standards visible

Once you've created the standards, they need to be visible. There are many ways to do this. From a laminated handout to a pocket card. From mousepads and screensavers to posters in the tearoom. It needs to be a living, breathing document the team sees daily. Every person in the organisation should have a copy of the service standards from day one. Talk about the standards in the recruitment and selection phase.

Include standards on their first day, orientation and onboarding

Service standards are critical for orientation and onboarding and underpin any customer service training program.

When a new team member joins an organisation, it is a prime opportunity to establish a service mindset. Go through the standards in detail on day one. Regardless of their previous experience, this is the time to orient the team around 'How we do things around here'. Give them a copy of the service standards and explain why it matters to bring these to life in their daily work. Service standards should then form part of the formal orientation and onboarding process. This should be for every employee in the organisation.

I was engaged to deliver a training program that commenced with the launch of the new standards the team had created. One of the frontline team was very excited when she first read them, saying, 'These should be our bible. These standards need to be part of our induction. Everyone should have a copy!' I couldn't have said it any better myself.

Every customer service training program needs the service standards woven into the content. They should be an underpinning foundation of any customer service training program, both initial and ongoing.

Coach service standards

One of the most significant advantages of clearly defined standards is that they can be used in service coaching. Effective service coaching is about improving behaviours, and the best way to do this is to link them to the service standards. Once the standards are defined, if a team member does not demonstrate the behaviours you wish to see, it is a perfect opportunity to provide coaching and feedback.

Recognise and celebrate success

In the memorable words of Ken Blanchard, leaders want to 'catch them doing something right'. When you see the team or individuals living and breathing the service standards in their daily work, acknowledge them. Acknowledge the behaviours you want to see more of, whether verbally or in writing. Tailoring the recognition to service standards is an important part of embedding behaviours.

Reinforce service standards

Once you've defined, trained, coached and recognised the standards, reinforcement builds the service culture. Do this through daily huddles, team meetings and catchups. Make sure the standards are not just seen at induction and training. They are a way of life.

The best example I have ever seen of reinforcing service standards is the Ritz-Carlton Hotel. Having studied them for many years, I am a raving fan of the Ritz-Carlton, and recently visited one of their hotels. In the words of Diana Oreck from Ritz-Carlton's Leadership Center: 'The daily line-up is the most important vehicle we have at Ritz-Carlton to keep culture alive. Every single day, 365 days a year, three times a day (because there are three different shifts), we have our line-up, and we cover the sixteen principles that are central to our service culture in rotation.'

During these daily line-ups, the leader reads the standard, then shares a story or customer feedback and team members also contribute.

Just ten minutes a day. Every day of the year.

This is what commitment to excellence looks like — ongoing reinforcement and a way to emphasise what was taught beyond the initial orientation and training. It is also why the Ritz-Carlton Hotel is world-famous for its guest experiences. It is deeply embedded in the culture and reinforced every single day.

The daily line-up is undoubtedly one of the best tools a leader has to connect and engage the team and reinforce what is required to deliver an exceptional customer experience in a positive and uplifting way. This can be done face-to-face and in virtual environments. Keeping service standards alive is a primary role of every service leader. As Taiichi Ohno, the father of the Toyota Production System, said, 'Without standards, there can be no improvement'.

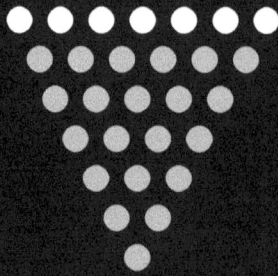

Chapter Summary

Practical tips

- Have clear, documented service standards in place. If they don't exist, create them.

- When you create service standards, use customer input and feedback, team input and leadership input. The standards need to be clear, specific, observable and measurable.

- Ensure the senior leadership and executive sign off the standards before socialisation.

- Make standards visible and ensure each team member has a copy.

- Review service standards every twelve months to ensure they are still relevant. Update accordingly.

Reflection questions

- Do you have service standards in place?

- Does your team know what your service standards are?

- How do you link service standards to recognition?

- How do you use the standards in ongoing coaching?

- How do you reinforce the standards on a daily and weekly basis?

Actions to take:

Chapter Six

Recruit People with Service in their Souls

'The most important thing you can do as a leader is to hire the right people.'

– David Cottrell

'You have to recruit people with service in their souls.'

Recruitment and careful selection are critical parts of the employee journey. So much of the customers' experience is determined by getting the recruitment process right in the first place.

Beyond recruiting the team, recruiting service leaders is pivotal in building a service culture. Leadership is often the heart and soul behind a customer-focused team and organisation, from hiring the CEO and the executive to all people leaders. Organisations must prioritise identifying and hiring leaders in every department of the business to drive a strong service culture, care for and motivate their team and help people to be the best they can be.

We often hear the saying, 'Hire for attitude, train for skills'. Notwithstanding that, certain roles require specific qualifications and skills. You would never recruit a pilot who didn't know how to fly an aeroplane. However, placing the right person with the right attitude and finding people who truly want to care for customers makes a significant difference to everyone. Thoughtful recruitment processes can also be a key differentiator in attracting and retaining talent.

Square pegs in round holes

Some years ago, I ran a public training workshop attended by people from a range of organisations. The program was called 'Exceptional Customer Service' and I loved delivering it. One particular day, I was setting up the room when the first person arrived. I introduced myself and we had a chat. After a minute, she said, 'I can't believe I'm here. I hate customers. I hate talking to them. I hate interacting with them. I can't stand dealing with people.' While I was a little taken aback, I was keen to explore the conversation further, so I asked, 'That's really interesting. What do you do at your company?' Her answer? 'I'm the receptionist.'

Think about the role of the receptionist in any organisation. It's one of the most critical, customer-facing roles, responsible for welcoming and greeting customers and often creating first impressions. And she genuinely did not want to be there to look after the customer.

This story is not about judgement. It was a classic example of bad job fit and poor recruitment practices. The organisation had sent her to the training program to try and fundamentally change who she was. It didn't matter what I talked about or what skills we focused on; a one-day training program was not going to make her love working with customers.

We spent some time together during the break, discussing her interests and preferences and exploring other more enjoyable and suitable roles that were less involved with customer interaction. I encouraged her to go back and speak to her leader about different possibilities and her needs and preferences for work.

The cost of the wrong role

Getting the wrong person for the job in customer service is very time-consuming and can be very costly. In a survey of more than 1500 HR professionals from Australia and New Zealand, ELMO Software, in partnership with the Australian HR Institute, found that the cost to hire an employee more than doubled in 2021, rising from AU$10,500 in 2020 to AU$23,860 per worker.[9]

And that is just the cost of hiring. The cost of training and onboarding a wrong hire can be enormous. It can impact the team, morale and motivation and the customer experience. Hiring the right people in customer-facing roles and setting them up for success is essential for your organisation's long-term strength.

As a service leader, how do you hire people who can build positive customer relationships, deliver that human touch and create exceptional customer service experiences? Hiring the right people is the first step in service excellence. That is why the Service Profit Chain lists it as one of the first elements of internal service quality.

Often, the role of a service leader involves recruitment at some level, be it solely their responsibility or with the help and support of People and Culture/Human Resources or an outsourced specialist recruitment firm. Recruitment is a specialist skill, and having the right expertise can help secure the right person for the role.

I have always maintained that working in customer service is not for the faint-hearted. The role takes a special type of person. It can be demanding, exhilarating, rewarding and challenging all at once. There are many skills and qualities required to be successful in service. While artificial intelligence and automation have removed many simple tasks, when a customer needs a real person to speak to, they are looking for high levels of connection, empathy and engagement.

The level of thought and time that goes into hiring the right person makes a difference. Consider who will fit well into your team and culture and align with your organisational values and purpose. You also need to consider what kind of person could do the role and identify the required skills and experience. What does the role demand? What qualities and technical skills are essential? Be very clear about what you are looking for.

Hollie Delaney, the former head of Human Resources at Zappos, says, 'First off, we take our time. After all, if our employees are our greatest resource, it only makes sense that we would put some serious effort into finding the right humans for our company.'

Identify the skills and attributes you are looking for

While it can depend on the role, some fundamental attributes are essential when working with customers.

Empathy

In a post-pandemic world of increasing automation, artificial intelligence and self-service, the way customers engage with organisations is also changing. They can (and often prefer to) do many actions for themselves, having built the confidence to embrace self-service. Customers across all generations are willingly turning to chatbots to resolve simple problems.

However, they look to engage with empathetic team members with advanced problem-solving skills for more complex issues. The human connection becomes so much more powerful. According to Zendesk, 'Demonstrating empathy and making better connections with customers to help them solve their problems has become a differentiator for successful companies.'[10]

A leader once asked me an incredibly insightful question. 'Can you teach someone to be empathetic?' I have long been fascinated by this question, and the answer is complex. Maia Szalavitz and Bruce Perry's book, *Born for Love: Why Empathy is Essential - And Endangered,* explores how and why our brains learn to bond with others.[11] Their work shows how compassion underlies the qualities that make our society work (trust, altruism, collaboration, love, charity) and how difficulties related to empathy are key factors in social problems.

Given the complexity of developing empathy, I have found some helpful tools to teach the skill in customer interactions. These include empathy mapping, reading customers' emotions, and developing authentic, empathetic language. The ability to validate customers' emotions and express empathy through language is essential for team members dealing with increasingly complex customer interactions.

In writing for Business Insider, Doug Clinton said, 'As the automation age eliminates rote and some not-so-rote tasks, it will create an opportunity for humans to capitalize on empathy. The manifestation of empathy in industry is through unique and memorable customer service, no matter the business.'[12]

Problem-solving

Advanced problem-solving and the ability to pinpoint the issue and find a resolution are vital to working effectively with customers. This includes creative problem-solving, which is often the ability to look for what is not said and analyse and research customer problems.

Resilience

Customer service involves high levels of customer contact, often with minimal time between interactions and handling multiple tasks at once. At a time when many customers have high levels of stress, customer service work is even more challenging. Workloads are heavier, responsibilities are increasing, people shortages are impacting many industries and difficult customer behaviour is increasing. Since the outbreak of COVID-19, Australian retailers have reported that aggression and abuse have increased by as much as 400%.[13]

The ability to be resilient and bounce back from difficult encounters is essential in customer service. However, this must be supported by leadership with a strong focus on care for the team, which includes de-briefing and access to external counselling services for serious incidents.

Positive attitude

Anyone who has worked a day in customer service knows the importance of attitude. It takes a massive amount of skill, knowledge and expertise to work with customers, show up every day and be present and customer-focused. I have always maintained that a positive attitude is one of the most important things to bring to work. Yet this is not always easy when dealing with high volumes of customer contact, circumstances outside work and the daily challenges we face managing multiple demands at work and home. Self-aware team members who can self-manage and demonstrate high levels of emotional intelligence are more successful working with customers.

Conflict resolution

The ability to resolve conflict and deal with difficult situations is another vital part of working in a customer service role. If people are conflict-averse, this part of the role becomes even more challenging. While we can provide training and support, problem-solvers who are willing to do whatever they can to turn customer dissatisfaction into satisfaction are a tremendous asset to the team, as they see difficult situations as a challenge and an opportunity. They can remain calm and in control even when the customer is not.

Communication skills

Superior communication skills are essential to work effectively with customers. Working in service requires people to adapt to customers with different communication style preferences, cultures and backgrounds. This is coupled with the ability to deal with customers via various communication channels, including face-to-face, written, social media or live chat, depending on the role. Active listening is essential to understanding customers' needs, wants and concerns.

Adaptability

With new and constantly changing technology, we want people who are willing to learn and develop in a fast-moving environment. While a new team member can be taught the tools, products, processes and technology, the ability to manage the customer in such an environment is why a willingness to learn and adapt is greatly valued.

Caring

Customer service is a people-focused job. Ultimately, a genuine desire to help people is the key trait of a capable customer service team member. People who are friendly and caring and demonstrate that they enjoy helping customers and can do so every day are assets to any team.

Write a job description that attracts the right people

While defining the desired attributes is one part of candidate selection, so too is writing a job description that attracts the right people to the role. It should clearly outline the role and responsibilities and describe the service culture and commitment to the customer. There is currently a huge demand for talent, so write a job description that stands out and shows how much the organisation cares for its people and customers. Video is increasingly used as a creative way to discuss the role and filter the right people.

Conduct the interview

The interview is an essential part of the employee experience and journey. It is an opportunity to discuss the importance of the customer to the organisation and introduce the service culture.

Situational and behavioural questions are commonly asked in interviews to understand how and why candidates have approached and responded to various scenarios. These are designed to tap into the candidate's experience and typically start with 'Tell me about a time when...?' or 'Can you share an example...?'.

Past behaviour can be a strong predictor of future performance. A candidate's answers can help an employer understand how well they will likely perform. That means asking the right questions is critical.

Many organisations have an in-depth approach to their selection process. For example, Four Seasons is an international luxury chain of hotels and resorts renowned for its customer experience. They take hiring very seriously. Each vacant position takes a minimum of four separate job interviews to fill. The chain developed an intensive interview process to recruit employees with the right attitudes to provide continuous five-star customer service. While skills are important for potential applicants, the hotel focuses more on using interviews to identify candidates dedicated to providing world-class care and service to guests.

Setting clear expectations, communication and follow-up are part of the post-interview experience. In a competitive job market, this part of the experience is essential.

Offer the role

Just like touchpoints in the customer journey, offering the role is an opportunity to show the candidate you care. Respond to them promptly, and be enthusiastic and passionate when offering the role to make them feel valued.

Use sensitivity and care with unsuccessful candidates and consider how they may feel. Often both parties have put a lot of time and effort into the selection process, so think about how to deliver the news with empathy and care. This can be an opportunity to educate and inform the candidate and help them prepare for future interviews through proactive and constructive feedback. Make it a positive experience with your organisation.

It is important not to rush hiring decisions. Getting the right people in place to care for your customers ultimately saves an enormous amount of time, effort, energy and headaches. There is a financial and human cost to re-hiring and re-training people. If you select carefully, they will tend to stay as they will be a right fit for the job and enjoy what they do. This will flow through to all customer interactions.

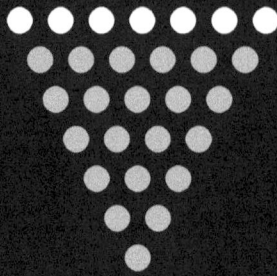

Chapter Summary

Practical tips

- Review the end-to-end recruitment journey for candidates. Make a list of required skills and attributes for each role and use situational and behavioural questions in every interview.

- Look for candidates who are passionate about customer service.

- Find creative ways to share vacant positions that represent your service culture.

- Be proactive in contacting People and Culture /Human Resources for additional expertise and support.

- Ensure the process of offering roles is timely in a competitive job market. Care for unsuccessful candidates with empathy and sensitivity.

Reflection questions

- What is the recruitment experience like for candidates who apply for roles in your organisation?

- Do you feel confident in your skills in recruitment and selection, or is this an area you could develop further?

- Do you rush recruitment decisions because of pressure to fill the role, or do you take time to get the right person?

Actions to take:

Chapter Seven

The First Day, Orientation, Onboarding and Development

'Onboarding starts with satisfying the most basic of Maslow's psychological needs: belonging. New hires shouldn't arrive to an empty cube and be forced to forage through corridors searching for a computer and the bare necessities of office life. A new hire isn't a surprise visitor from out of town. Plan for their arrival.'

– Jay Samit

How a team member is welcomed into an organisation has a long-term impact on how they feel about the organisation. This begins on their first day and continues throughout the formal orientation and longer-term onboarding process.

The day-one experience

The new team member's first day is a one-off, never-to-be-repeated opportunity to create a memorable experience for the team member, and it starts with how the leader welcomes them.

I once read that no one is ever as attentive as on their first day. So, as a service leader, consider the following.

'How do I make their first day magical?'

Even before their first day, make a phone call to say hello and let the team member know how excited you are that they are joining the team. Confirm where to meet or start and give them an idea of what to expect on their first day. These all show thoughtful consideration before they commence.

Ask yourself what you want their first day to be like. How do you want them to feel? What do you want them to say at the end of their first day?

Can you remember how you felt on the first day of your job?

Over the years, I have heard far too many horror stories of team members turning up to reception with no one there, being left waiting at reception, taken to a desk with a computer and then left alone for a couple of days. One of the worst stories I ever heard was of a team member who spent their first day 'buddying' with one of the company's most disgruntled and negative team members, cleaning out his van and saying how much he despised the company they worked for. The day-one experience stays with us for a long time and can impact how valued we feel.

A service leader takes this responsibility seriously and ensures all elements of the first day are ready before the team member's arrival. That includes having computers, passwords and access to systems organised and perhaps a welcome pack or gift. Preparation is the cornerstone of successful onboarding.

When a new team member arrives on their first day, a service leader should be waiting in reception to greet them. It's like welcoming a special guest at a five-star hotel. Arrange for the new person to meet the rest of the team and key stakeholders. It could be a welcome morning tea or a one-on-one lunch, depending on whether it is a single hire or welcoming several team members. It is all about intentionally creating the experience for them. I ask leaders to consider what they want the team member to say when they arrive home after their first day. Will they be excited about returning the next day, confident they have made the right decision?

In the new world of work, not all inductions will be in person, so additional thought is necessary for virtual first days, orientations and onboarding experiences. The same principles apply, with consideration about fostering human connection and making it engaging and memorable, albeit virtual. Perhaps you can send the welcome pack to the team member's home or have their favourite coffee or lunch delivered to their doorstep. It takes care, consideration and creativity to make a virtual first day unforgettable!

Orientation

The company orientation formally welcomes new team members into the organisation. This can take anywhere from a half-day to a week and is often delivered in person as an event with various people from different departments attending. It is often facilitated by HR and is a chance for the team member to be inspired by the organisation's mission, values, history and purpose.

A well-planned orientation should be engaging, inspiring and a chance to immerse the person in the service culture. It should never be a series of PowerPoint slides that will put them to sleep. Design the orientation to create connection, fun, engagement and pride in joining the company. You want people to leave excited and energised, knowing they have made the right decision and built new connections across the organisation.

The company orientation must have a specific and dedicated customer service element. This extends to those working directly on the frontline with customers and every team member and leader — whether they work in customer service, IT, human resources or finance or as the CEO, director or leader. Everyone attends the same customer service component of orientation, which is the perfect opportunity to introduce service standards.

I strongly advocate that people at all levels of the organisation should spend time in customer service on the frontline or listening to calls as part of the orientation or onboarding process. There is no better way to build empathy for customer service than to hear the voice of the customer directly.

One of my favourite examples of this is Zappos. Their four-week induction program covers the company's history, the importance of customer service and the long-term vision of the company. Everyone spends two weeks in the call centre, taking calls from customers. And that means all leaders and team members, whether they're customer-facing or not. Tony Hsieh, the former CEO of Zappos, said, 'Customer service is not a department. It should be the entire company.' The program was designed to bring this statement to life.

I recall my induction at Optus many years ago. As a customer service representative, we had four weeks of training, including a week on customer service and an overnight retreat called the 'Optus Challenge'. That experience set me up for success and was one of the reasons for such a strong customer service culture within the organisation. I came home bubbling with excitement and shared my positive stories with my mother. She listened patiently as I spoke for an hour, then looked at me and said, 'You have been Optusised!'. This experience was over twenty-five years ago, yet I remember it like it was yesterday.

I speak to far too many team members across multiple industries where there is either no orientation or the customer is not even mentioned in their orientation. If we truly want to enable our people, set our teams up for success, and build strong customer service cultures, it all starts with how we design their orientation and onboarding experience. And the orientation component is only a small piece of the onboarding pie.

Onboarding

Onboarding is the strategic process of immersing the new team member into their role, the organisation and culture. It is tailored and customised for each individual and their role and typically can take up to twelve months.

Every service leader is responsible for a formalised and well-considered onboarding process for each team member. It involves ongoing development in the workplace and is leader-led. Onboarding can significantly improve employee engagement and reduce turnover.

It is an important time to discuss realistic expectations about how long it can take to become confident in the role. Depending on the complexity of the products or the organisation, it can feel daunting for the team member when they first join. Reassure the team member and let them know they may feel overwhelmed to begin with, but the onboarding process will ensure they will become confident and competent over time. Some team members will have very high expectations of themselves and may feel frustrated at how long it takes to adjust to a new role. A reassuring leader will make all the difference.

According to UrbanBound, UK and US companies spend US$37 billion annually to retain unproductive employees who don't understand their jobs. In contrast, amazingly, 35% of those companies spend $0 on onboarding.[14]

Consider the time and effort it takes to recruit and select a team member.

All of this is wasted unless there is effective onboarding. Poor onboarding puts performance, retention and customer experience at risk. Only 29% of new hires say they feel fully prepared and supported to excel in their role after their onboarding experience.[15] This is an alarming statistic given the current demand for talent and, more importantly, how people feel about their ability to succeed in their roles.

Give particular consideration to helping remote workers develop workplace relationships and learn their role in a virtual setting. This has changed significantly post-pandemic, as with virtual work becoming the new normal, many teams are not physically together. I recently worked with an amazing team that physically came together for the first time in three years.

Onboarding is about creating human connections and ensuring people know how they will contribute to the team and organisation in person or virtually. It must be an organisational and leadership priority.

The onboarding process may also be when people realise a role is not for them. While (in theory) this should have been discovered in the recruitment and selection phase, other reasons could be a cultural misalignment or wrong job fit. Zappos gives new employees four weeks to decide if it's a good fit, then lets them quit and receive a month's pay. Such is the emphasis on getting the right culture and ensuring the right people are in place to take care of the customer.

Once you have attracted and hired the right people, it is essential to have an onboarding experience that makes team members feel welcome, valued and prepared and confirms they have made the right decision. The benefits of effective onboarding include reduced turnover, decreased stress, higher engagement and job satisfaction, long-term loyalty and commitment and a positive customer experience.

Development

*'Train people well enough so
they can leave, treat them well
enough so they don't want to.'*

– Richard Branson

Ongoing training and development must be about investment in the team member and their learning, expanding skills, aligning training with identified skill gaps, technology training and customer service refresher training. Training can be a powerful medium when there is proof that the root cause of the learning need is an undeveloped skill or a knowledge deficit.[16] It is never training for the sake of training. It needs to be targeted, relevant, meaningful and designed to help team members develop in their roles.

Beyond onboarding, the ongoing development of team members includes formal training, on-the-job training and practice. It may also comprise secondment opportunities and acting team leader roles and should be tailored for each individual depending on their training and development needs and future aspirations.

David McCarthy was one of my first team leaders when I worked as a customer service representative. David, or 'Macca' as he was fondly known, was a passionate advocate for his team. He knew each of our career goals and did everything he could to help us to develop. Under his guidance, I was able to do volunteer work with the training department. Knowing this was the direction I wanted to go, he fully supported me to return to university part-time to study training and development. I now look back at our induction group '47M' and appreciate how much Macca helped so many of our team reach their career goals.

While onboarding begins team member development, ongoing development is essential. It's useful to know this during the recruitment phase. Some people will prefer to stay in customer service roles, while others will have different aspirations. From the original team I worked with, one team member has happily spent twenty years working on the phones as a customer service team member. He still loves his role, while another ended up in a senior HR leadership position.

Hiring from within and developing people for future roles can really benefit the organisation. Look for people you can nurture and promote. Advocate for your team. Customer service can be an incredible source of talent for the organisation. The level of expertise, skills, organisational knowledge and experience they gain working with customers is transferable to many other departments within the company. Recruiting from within benefits the team member and their development, as well as the customer experience.

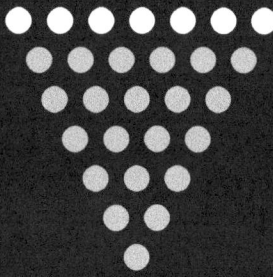

Chapter Summary

Practical tips

- Ensure customer service is part of your corporate orientation. Offer to speak at orientation to ensure customer service has a voice!

- Arrange opportunities for new hires to sit with customer service and listen to calls.

- Provide a well-planned first-day experience and a structured orientation and onboarding plan for all team members.

- Make time to find out the career aspirations of your team members and incorporate this into their development plan. Support them in reaching their goals and aspirations.

- Conduct regular cadence calls with each new team member to see how they are progressing. This should form part of the 12-month onboarding plan.

Reflection questions

- What is the first day like for people joining your team? How do they feel at the end of day one?

- What is the orientation and onboarding process for new team members?

- Do you have a defined development plan for each person?

Actions to take:

Chapter Eight

Retention

'If you are lucky enough to be someone's employer, then you have a moral obligation to make sure people do look forward to coming to work in the morning.'

– John Mackey

Employee retention is an organisation's ability to retain its current employees. There is a strong correlation between a team member having a positive experience in the workplace and their intent to stay. Retaining talent is integral to an organisation's long-term success as well as the customer experience.

There are significant costs associated with turnover aside from recruiting and retraining. It can impact the customer, and before people physically leave, they may 'check out', resulting in lower engagement, reduced productivity and morale.

According to experience management company Qualtrics XM, engaged employees are 87% less likely to leave their organisation. That means reduced turnover costs in recruiting and training new staff and less lag time between training and full productivity.[17] It also results in improved outcomes and performance, lower attrition, increased revenue and improved customer experience.

Employee retention is closely linked to employee experience, and there are strategies an organisation can employ to help people want to stay.

It is important to reflect on what makes people want to leave. While a certain level of attrition is normal, other reasons for leaving could have been avoided. These include team members not feeling valued, misaligned values, poor leadership, burnout and leaders not taking action or listening to feedback. People also leave if there is no development path or a more attractive external opportunity arises. As a service leader, consider how you can proactively retain talent.

While much has been written about the Great Resignation and Quiet Quitting, retaining talent must remain an overarching priority for every organisation.

Strategies for increasing retention

Here are some ways that you can support people to stay.

Conduct stay interviews

I love the concept of 'stay' interviews. So many organisations focus on exit interviews rather than proactively reaching out to team members to ask if they are happy, spend time exploring their career goals and ensure they are satisfied and happy at work.

In her book, *The 7 Intuitive Laws of Employee Loyalty*, Heather R. Younger writes, 'There is a growing trend toward conducting employee-stay interviews in place of, or in addition to, exit interviews. This is primarily due to unsuccessful attempts to gather trustworthy feedback from people on their way out the door. It turns out that current employees are much more likely to give human resources the time of day and even sit to talk about the work environment. Also, they are more likely to provide balanced feedback.'[18]

Whether at the start or end of the year, check in regularly with the team.

Listen to and act on feedback

Listening to and acting on feedback is so significant that I've dedicated Chapter Thirteen to the voice of the team. Creating formal and informal opportunities to listen and act on feedback is one of the most important roles of a service leader and has a massive impact on retention. Management thinker Roger Martin explains it well. 'Never dismiss their ideas, never allow their progress to be blocked, and never miss the chance to shower them with praise when they succeed.'[19]

Offer flexible work

If COVID-19 has taught us anything, it is the need to offer flexible working conditions for team members, with far more creativity around hours and roles that suit them. And that includes remote and hybrid roles. Some parts of customer service have particular requirements to enable customer coverage which means specific working hours and conditions. These are important considerations in initial recruitment and selection discussions.

A PricewaterhouseCoopers (PWC) survey found that 45% of respondents who are unable to work from home reported less job satisfaction than their colleagues who can. Fifty per cent of employees surveyed said being able to choose where to work was the most important factor when deciding whether to change jobs.[20]

Engage the team in professional development

A lack of visible professional development or career progression can be a significant reason people leave to pursue other opportunities. This development conversation needs to be had with each team member to know their goals and expectations and keep them informed regarding their career progression. I have heard too many examples of people leaving the organisation for a new role, only to be told (too late) they were being considered for a promotion or other opportunities. Don't lose good people through lack of communication.

Prevent burnout and promote wellbeing

Nothing should be more important for organisations than the care and wellbeing of employees. It's not about the impact on customers or productivity; this is the human cost with implications for mental health. UK employee engagement statistics from 2021 suggest that burned-out employees are 63% more likely to take a sick day and 2.6 times more likely to look for another job.[21] Stress at work also affects relationships outside of work.

Maslach, Jackson and Leiter have identified six leading causes of burnout: unsustainable workload, perceived lack of control, insufficient rewards for effort, lack of a supportive community, lack of fairness and mismatched values and skills.[22]

An observant leader can have a significant role in preventing burnout and focusing on wellbeing. It's not about promoting self-care as a band-aid solution; instead, it is a commitment from the organisation to workplace practices and support to avoid it becoming an issue in the first place. The focus is on prevention, not cure.

Create a sense of belonging

Belonging can be defined as 'the experience of being seen and heard and welcome with all of who we are'.[23]

Ensuring people feel valued and belong to the team and organisation has a real impact on retention. Social belonging is a fundamental human need. Have you ever attended a party or function where you did not feel welcome? Our bodies are wired to scan for threats or dangers, and our first instinct is often to remove ourselves from uncomfortable situations. The same applies to workplaces. People are likely to leave if they feel they don't belong.

High belonging was linked to a whopping 56% increase in job performance, a 50% drop in turnover risk, and a 75% reduction in sick days. Employees with higher workplace belonging also showed a 167% increase in their employer promoter score (eNPS) which is their willingness to recommend their company to others.[24]

Prioritise diversity, equity and inclusion

Creating a workplace of belonging starts with creating psychologically safe workplaces, inclusive leadership and focusing on diversity, equity and inclusion.

When employees feel included, involved and accepted (real inclusion), they feel they belong in the workplace.[25] There is a strong correlation between a sense of belonging and organisations that are committed in actions (not just words) to diversity, equity and inclusion. Being progressive in this space for both employees and customers will likely retain and attract talent.

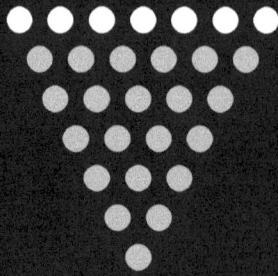

Chapter Summary

Practical tips

- Conduct 'stay' interviews with the team. These could be at the start or end of the year or as part of ongoing conversations.

- Ensure there is a professional development and career plan in place for each team member.

- Have strategies in place to prevent workplace burnout and promote wellbeing. This should include a comprehensive plan for managing mental health.

Reflection questions

- What do you currently have in place to listen and learn from feedback?

- As an organisation and a leader, how do you prioritise the prevention of burnout and proactively promote wellbeing?

- Are you fully aware of the career aspirations of everyone in your team?

Actions to take:

Chapter Nine

Off-boarding

*'I've learned that people will forget
what you said, people will forget
what you did, but people will never
forget how you made them feel.'*

– Maya Angelou

A positive off-boarding or exit experience is an integral part of the employee journey.

Team members leave a team or organisation for many reasons, whether voluntary or involuntary. These could include another internal opportunity, a new external role, retirement, redundancy or (in a different set of circumstances and approach) a termination. As with customer service, we talk about the power of first and last impressions and consider how you want the team member to feel when they leave the organisation.

There can also be a range of emotions in how a team member may feel about leaving, from excitement about a new role to the dread or joy of retirement. Redundancy is universally considered traumatic, even if there is a favourable financial outcome or ongoing post-job placement support.

The off-boarding experience needs careful design. One study found that 71% of organisations have no formal off-boarding process.[26] This poses an obvious risk to the human experience and significantly increases financial, legal and security risks.

Steps in off-boarding

From a logistical perspective, certain steps need to be considered, including organising the replacement of the departing team member or organising a thorough handover to minimise the impact on the customer. There is also an opportunity to demonstrate care and make the off-boarding experience positive. A service leader takes the following steps.

Communicate the news to the team

Informing the team about why the person is leaving is important for everyone. Make the communication open and transparent. How this is delivered, the message and the timing will depend on the reason for the departure.

Sort the paperwork

There is always paperwork associated with any departure, including forms, final pay and financials, and IT. Organise this before they leave. Give yourself adequate time to prepare and liaise with various departments to ensure everything is done on time. Leaving things to the last minute puts stress and pressure on you, the team member and internal departments.

Organise knowledge transfer

When someone leaves the team, there will always be a loss of that person's knowledge and expertise. You may need to train another team member to ensure a thorough handover of a client portfolio. That is also why collecting and distributing knowledge throughout an employee's tenure is important.

Conduct the exit interview

Exit interviews may be in-person or online, each with pros and cons. In-person or phone interviews can enable more in-depth qualitative data, while an online survey may mean the team member feels they can be more candid or direct. In most cases, it is best not to have the direct manager conduct the exit interview, as this may inhibit the responses. What is most important, as well as the questions asked, is what happens to the data.

Studying exit interviews and discovering why people are leaving can help reduce unnecessary turnover. It can also help coach leaders if feedback has identified development opportunities. Exit interviews are important for people to feel heard, but only conduct them if the organisation pays attention to the results. Otherwise, it is a complete waste of everyone's time and effort.

Collect any company assets

Organising the collection of phones, laptops, security access cards, credit cards and any other artefacts is an integral part of the process, particularly from a security perspective. It is simply due diligence for any organisation.

Organise the celebration

The options are endless, from a well-considered gift, to a lunch or dinner, a card that everyone has signed, or a video of memories and messages. Make their last day as special as their first. Give particular consideration to those leaving involuntarily (especially with redundancies) and be sensitive about any celebration.

My late father was only fifty years old when he was suddenly made redundant from one of the leading four banks in Australia. Dad, and many of his similarly aged colleagues, were replaced with young managers who had never worked in a bank. The organisation changed their way of recruiting managers and, in the process, removed many managers with significant experience.

After thirty-three years of loyal service, it was difficult for Dad to comprehend what was happening. Suddenly being removed from a role he held dear was extraordinarily difficult. He loved his customers and team, and they all loved him. It was very traumatic, and Dad had no idea what the future held. With a family and associated responsibilities, it was a very intense time with much stress and worry.

After all those years of service, he was distressed about how he was treated. He had moved his young family multiple times for various roles at the bank's request and had done everything that was asked of him. After all that service, he was given a box to pack up his belongings and, in a matter of days, his career with the bank came to a close.

What I remember most from this time was the response from his customers and his team. As his branch was attached to a hospital, his customers were predominantly nurses, doctors and health professionals. The focus of Dad's customers was saving lives, and Dad did everything he could to make their lives easier with banking and their accounts. They trusted him and his care. So, when they learnt that he had been made redundant, they were devastated. They started writing letters and calling head office, demanding that he be reinstated. It got to the point where the bank asked Dad to tell his customers to stop calling. The thing was, Dad hadn't asked them to call; they did this of their own accord.

While the bank did nothing to farewell him in a caring manner, the customers arranged a beautiful send-off that meant the world to my Dad. His customers took turns speaking about Dad and what he had meant to them. His team also organised a separate beautiful farewell that showed their regard for him.

Dad treated everyone equally, whether it was the top cardiologist in the country, the security team or the people who cleaned the bank. He knew them personally, and they loved it. He knew people by name and got to know their stories. He knew about their kids and was as interested in his customers as his team. They were grateful for his incredible service and how he cared for them. Dad was deeply valued by his team and customers over many years of service.

When people leave an organisation, they deserve better than the bank's treatment of my father.

During one of my service leadership workshops, I heard the story of a completely different sendoff. One leader spoke about a company he had worked with during the pandemic lockdown in Melbourne. Given the restrictions, everyone worked from home, so he had never met the team in person. It was difficult to get everyone together for a traditional farewell. So his leader sent a chain letter around to each team member, and everybody wrote about the contribution he had made to the team. He shared that the letter is a treasured possession he carries with him always. It means more than anything he has ever received at work.

It is not always about a tangible gift; it is the level of thought and consideration that goes into the exit experience.

The departure of a team member is an important time to celebrate their contribution and ensure people leave feeling valued and appreciated. Celebrate this milestone whether they are choosing to take an external career opportunity or for any other reason.

As Ben Wigert and Sangeeta Agrawal explained, 'When an employee looks back at their time with you, they want to feel like it mattered. Every person wants to feel that they contributed, even in a small way.'[27]

Every service leader must think about the employee experience and journey from beginning to end to make it a positive, memorable and valued experience and remove any pain points and obstacles along the way.

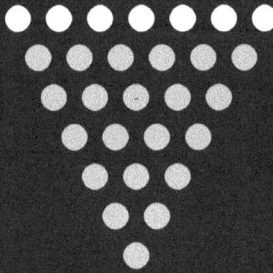

Chapter Summary

Practical tips

- Map out the off-boarding process and ensure all elements of off-boarding are covered.

- Learn from exit interview feedback about what can be improved.

- Be thoughtful and creative in organising celebrations and send-offs.

Reflection questions

- Who is responsible for exit interviews in your organisation? How do you learn as an organisation and leader from the data captured?

- How do you effectively capture knowledge so it is not lost when a team member leaves?

- What is the current off-boarding experience like for someone in your organisation or team?

Actions to take:

Chapter Ten

Give People the Tools to Serve Customers

'Giving great service requires the right people and the right service tools.'

– Ron Kaufman

It is my fundamental belief that no one turns up to work to deliver poor customer service. People don't wake up, get out of bed, get ready and head off to work thinking, 'I am going to deliver really bad service today'. In my many years of working with customer service teams, there are several reasons why a customer may not receive a positive experience, or poor service is delivered. Here are the most common reasons:

- poor processes
- technology issues
- lack of induction and training
- lack of coaching and feedback
- no standards or clear expectations for the team
- lack of tools to do the job
- poor leadership

- team member not suited to the job or role
- poor attitude.

Note that poor attitude is the least likely factor.

Every service leader must set their teams up for success, provide the best environment possible, and provide team members with the right tools to deliver exceptional customer experiences.

Imagine trying to build a house without the appropriate equipment. You could have the most incredible design and architecture, yet it would fail if the builders turned up without the right gear. They could have the best skills, attitude and mindset, but they would not be able to get the job done. The same can be said for customer service.

Give them what they need

I was asked to deliver telephone skills training to a team. Even though I had completed the pre-briefing scope, the leader indicated there were no issues I needed to be aware of.

You can imagine my shock and surprise when the team shot me down in flames before I even got through the session introduction. The team rightly questioned why I was presenting on telephone skills when the phone system didn't work. It constantly cut customers off, they couldn't transfer calls to other departments and the audio was horrific. Half the time, they couldn't even hear the customers, which made their jobs almost impossible.

They had raised this numerous times with their team leader and the manager I had met, yet nothing had changed. They were incredibly frustrated and at their wits' end from repeatedly having the same conversations. It was not their skill level, attitude or lack of wanting to help the customer. They didn't have poor telephone skills; they had an antiquated telephone system that frustrated and prevented them from doing the simplest tasks.

I spent the rest of the session empathising with the team and collating their feedback. I shared Stephen Covey's circles of concern and influence to help them focus on what they could control, influence and change. And yes, we shared some content about telephone skills.

After the training, I contacted the leader to share my findings, which, unfortunately, she instantly dismissed. She was not interested in hearing their feedback or how the inadequate phone system impacted the team and customer experience.

It was a perfect example of a lack of the right tools and technology impacting the teams' ability to serve the customer. The right tools and technology affect employee engagement, productivity and retention, as well as external service quality.

What are the right tools?

Many customer service tools and technologies can make the lives of those serving customers easier, including:

- telephone systems
- computers
- internal chat platforms to enable fast responses from coworkers and teams in other departments
- knowledge articles
- help desk software such as ticketing systems
- automation tools
- customer relationship management systems (CRM) to store

customer contact information and important notes about support requests

- webcams.

These should all focus on making things as effortless as possible for the team member, which, in turn, will make it easier for the customer.

From a leadership perspective, this can mean regularly checking in with the team to ensure the resources are working for them. For the service leader, it also means being a champion when things are not working for the team. That could involve conversations with senior leaders and putting a business case forward if new tools and technology are required.

I always advise service leaders to present a compelling business case that outlines customer effort, team effort, cost to serve, lost time, financial impact and even multiple handling of tasks. Technology changes are not quick fixes or overnight solutions and can be time-consuming and costly. If changes are planned, remember to keep the team updated about progress. Acknowledge their pain points and frustrations in the meantime.

Chapter Summary

Practical tips

- Make it a point to ask your team, 'What blocks or barriers are currently getting in the way of you delivering an excellent experience?' Ask for their solutions and ideas to overcome these barriers. This is an ideal activity to use in a team meeting or as a stand-alone facilitated session. Implement quick wins and create a plan for other ideas suggested.

- Review the tools, systems and processes the team have to do their jobs.

- Be an advocate for the team if tools and technology are hindering the team's ability to do its job and serve customers. Escalate to senior leadership where required.

Reflection questions

- Does your current technology serve or impede your team?

- Does your team have all the right tools to serve the customers?

- Are your processes both customer- and team-focused?

Actions to take:

Chapter Eleven

Accountability

*'Accountability is the glue that
ties commitment to the result.'*

– Bob Proctor

Accountability is at the heart of every customer-focused organisation, resulting in cultures where everyone genuinely cares about the customer and takes ownership. In customer service, it means each person takes responsibility and ownership for their decisions, actions, performance and behaviour.

Exceptional service leaders hold their teams accountable for results. Accountability is measuring each person's contributions according to recognised and accepted performance standards.

Accountability ensures that all metrics are tied back to the customer. Customer experience expert Jeanne Bliss says, 'Leadership accountability will come as people realise they are being judged on customer-centric metrics. They will evolve around to your ideas and positions. If they aren't judged on customer-facing elements, it will be a long battle uphill.' Accountability must be across all levels of the organisation — from the executive to the frontline and those in support roles.

Customer service accountability is a leadership mindset that may be present or absent for several reasons. Accountability is sometimes associated with micro-management and overbearing leaders who drive their teams into the ground. If this is the leader's behaviour, accountability will always be considered a dirty word. Importantly, the more influence and control people have over their work and results, the greater their accountability.

The Association for Talent Development studied accountability and found the following fascinating probabilities of success in completing a goal.[28]

- Having an idea or goal: 10%
- Consciously deciding that you will do it: 25%
- Deciding when you will do it: 40%
- Planning how to do it: 50%
- Committing to someone that you will do it: 65%
- Having a specific accountability appointment with someone you've committed to: 95%

These findings highlight the importance of keeping service goals in mind and the leadership accountability and follow-up to go with it.

Know what you're accountable for

So, how do we get everyone in our organisations to be accountable to and for the customer?

The most effective way is by ensuring everyone knows the expectations and setting clear goals. It is difficult to *be* accountable if we do not know what we are accountable *for*! Be clear on what success means to the customer, the team and the organisation.

Service leaders must drive accountability for the customer experience at three levels; leadership, frontline and internal.

Leadership accountability

Accountability for the customer experience is a leadership priority and ultimately impacts the customer experience.

In an organisation committed to building a strong service culture, the leadership team is accountable for the customer experience of their team in customer and non-customer facing roles. The CEO, executive, directors and people leaders across the organisation are all accountable for the customer. This understanding should be written into performance goals and metrics.

Leadership also holds the team accountable for customer outcomes, which is achieved by providing team members with the right training, support and empowerment to help the customer. Effective leaders look for ongoing ways to coach and develop their teams, provide feedback and recognise success.

Frontline accountability

For those working on the frontline, accountability is delivering on promises and taking ownership of the customer experience. It is responding to customer requests for information or help in a caring and efficient manner. Managing customer expectations, following up and providing ongoing communication are at the heart of all first-class service experiences. Accountability is delivering on service standards and commitments. Service leaders hold their teams to account and ensure they meet their customer goals and targets.

Internal accountability

It is not only the frontline that needs to be held accountable to the customer; this must also be driven through support roles and internal departments. Delivering a superior customer experience is virtually impossible without an internal focus on the customer and serving each other. Lack of internal accountability can lead to some departments contributing to poor responsiveness, lengthy resolution times and, ultimately, customer complaints. That is where cross-functional collaboration is essential, with clear expectations and standards set for internal teams. Leaders of internal teams need to drive internal customer accountability.

Think about the impact of the lack of accountability. Failure to be accountable for the customer at any level leads to poor customer service, performance, lower team engagement, re-work and complaints. Accountability in customer service has been linked to improved customer service and work performance, ease of customer experience, increased commitment to working, and improved morale and satisfaction.

When people are accountable for their own decisions, work and results, the effectiveness of an organisation can increase significantly. Accountability can be achieved by leading in a caring and humane way.

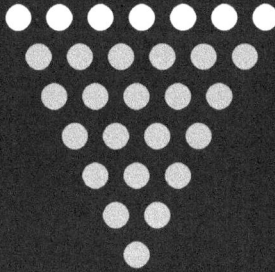

Chapter Summary

Practical tips

- Ensure customer-driven metrics and measures are specific, measurable and communicated to the team.

- Accountability for the customer experience must be in place for leaders, the frontline and internal support roles; otherwise, it will never be an organisational priority.

- Build a positive culture of accountability in your team and make time to celebrate success.

Reflection questions

- Is your team clear on what accountability for the customer experience looks like?

- How do you hold yourselves accountable as a team? How could you improve your accountability to each other?

- How do you hold yourself accountable as a leader?

- How could you improve internal customer accountability?

- Do you put our customers at the centre of your accountability actions? Do your processes help or hinder accountability?

Actions to take:

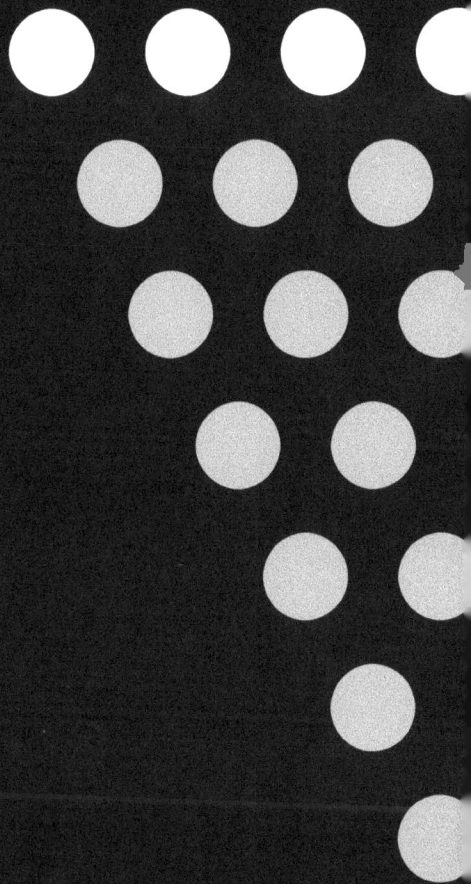

PART THREE
EMPOWER

Chapter Twelve

Empowerment

'Leadership is providing inspiration and vision, then developing and empowering others to achieve this vision.'

– Marshall Goldsmith

The ability of a service leader to empower their team is one of the most critical elements of the customer experience. It goes well beyond simply saying, 'You are empowered'. It is how we empower team members by ensuring they have the knowledge, authority and decision-making capability to act in the customer's and organisation's best interests.

There are many benefits of an empowered workforce. It positively impacts the team member, the customer and the leader. Knowing they have a supportive leader who will back them all the way encourages the team to generate creative ideas and think of new ways of doing things.

Empowerment is positively associated with a range of employee outcomes, including job satisfaction, organisational commitment, improved productivity, and reduced turnover and is linked to team performance and morale. The impact on the customer is also significant, resulting in quicker responses, reduced escalations and minimised customer frustration.

Disempowerment is costly

The most memorable example of the impact of empowerment I have ever seen was working on a large-scale customer transformation project with a top ASX-listed organisation. During our first scoping meeting, the director of Human Resources told me I was about to walk into the most 'broken' customer service culture I had ever seen. It wasn't far from the truth!

The initial scope was to improve the customer experience by providing training to the frontline. However, after our first meeting and from the data and learnings I captured, I recommended we start with the entire leadership team. Fortunately, I was working with a receptive senior leadership team who understood my thinking, and the outcome was that I conducted a two-day service leadership workshop with the top forty leaders in the company.

When we got to the module on empowerment, one leader stood bravely and told the group, 'I don't think our team feels empowered to help the customer.' The director of HR was a curious leader who genuinely listened, wanted to learn more and probed further. She asked the leader to share their thoughts and they proceeded to give examples. The list was very long.

One example related to the amount of money the team was permitted to spend to resolve a customer issue. The limit was $70. If the credit needed $70.50, a complex and time-consuming escalation path kicked in. They had to refer the customer case to a supervisor, which they had to escalate to their leader. Once reviewed by multiple layers of leadership, the decision would come back approved with the same outcome the team member would have made.

This restriction created enormous frustration for team members, customers and leaders. All because leaders spent so much time and energy trying to settle things that the team members could have easily resolved themselves. It was costly in terms of time and resources, let alone the impact on the customer experience and the number of customer complaints and escalations because of the time taken to resolve the issues.

This frustration was expressed even more deeply when I commenced training with the frontline and support teams.

One question I often ask teams, particularly in cultural change transformation projects, is, 'What blocks and barriers are getting in the way of you delivering an exceptional customer experience?' Unsurprisingly, this team's number one issue was lack of empowerment. It was loud and clear. The team said they did not feel at all empowered to help the customer as leaders had to approve everything. The escalation path was excruciating for everyone. This message was consistent in every workshop. I collected all the feedback and shared it with the senior leadership team.

The HR director listened and, most importantly, acted quickly on the feedback, initiating several changes. The discretionary spend of $70 was quadrupled and, in some cases, increased tenfold. They simplified the escalation path. And the result? Team members were happier. Customers were happier. And leaders were happier because they had more time. Complaints and escalations reduced and team morale and motivation improved out of sight. It was a powerful example of the difference empowering the frontline team can make on multiple levels and the importance of listening to and acting on feedback. It also illustrated how critical senior-level support is in facilitating empowerment and creating change.

The foundations of empowerment

Empowerment happens at three levels: knowledge, decision-making and discretionary spend.

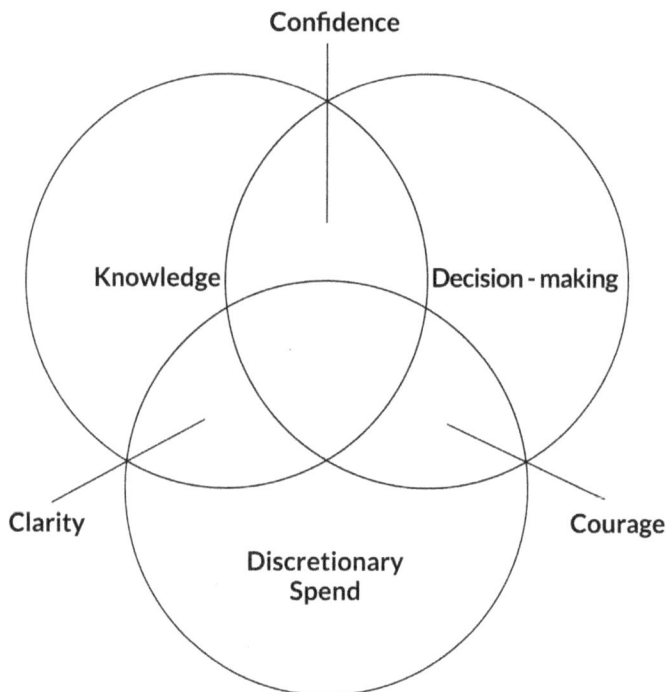

Confidence

Knowledge

Decision - making

Clarity

Courage

Discretionary
Spend

Figure 9: The model of empowerment

Knowledge

If a team member is empowered with knowledge, they are in a far better position to help the customer. This is one of the foundations of empowerment and why onboarding and ongoing training and development are so important. The team needs the knowledge to help the customer and create solutions and alternatives. That includes access to articles, quick access guides and internal tools. As one of my early team leaders told me,

'Don't try to remember everything; know where to find the information!' Knowledge is essential for a team member to feel empowered to help the customer.

Decision-making

Empowerment means every employee can make fast decisions in favour of the customer at every encounter. Leaders who are perceived as more empowering are more likely to delegate authority to their employees, ask for their input, and encourage autonomous decision-making.[1]

Every team member needs to know what decisions they can make and when to escalate to their leader.

Discretionary spend

Discretionary spend relates to how much the team member is authorised to spend before escalating to a leader for approval. While this will vary depending on the organisation and industry, it is a significant element of empowerment.

On a recent family holiday, I was at a shop at a theme park and was accidentally charged for four items instead of three. The total cost of the additional item was $4.50. The team member behind the counter told me she couldn't do the refund and would have to call her manager to authorise it. I waited patiently until the manager arrived and completed the refund.

That transaction is an example of dumb rules that get in the way of delivering exceptional service. The team member could have made this decision and easily arranged the refund herself. It is simply a matter of trust and empowerment. Empowerment is foremost when creating exceptional customer experiences and a more positive working experience for the team. I couldn't help but think of how much time and energy the process took for everyone involved. And that was a single transaction in a busy theme park. How many times a day does this scenario play out? In the words of Stephen M.R. Covey, 'People want to be trusted. It's the most compelling form of human motivation'.

As mentioned in Chapter Five, I am a huge fan of the Ritz-Carlton Hotel. It offers the best example of empowerment I have come across. Famous for how it takes care of its guests, it also has a strong focus on taking care of its people.

Every Ritz-Carlton team member, at every level, is empowered to spend up to $2,000 per guest per incident. The company reports that while the full amount (or more, with the general manager's permission) can be used, it rarely is.

When there is an incident, the team member is closest to the customer and can resolve the issue quicker. They can do this alone, without having to go through levels of leadership for approval which involves more time and cost. They are encouraged to devise memorable ways to elevate the guest experience.

Courage vs consequences

Your team will only make decisions in the customer's best interests if they have the courage to do so. I refer to this as the moment of courage vs consequences. If a team member feels trusted and empowered, they make a decision. They will never make these decisions if they fear reprisal, lack leadership support or are concerned that they will get into trouble.

A team feels supported and empowered if mistakes are viewed as a learning or coaching opportunity, and they know the leader will back them — no matter what. Empowering leadership is about mentoring and supporting employee development, so even if a team member does make a wrong decision, it is viewed purely as a learning opportunity.

The element of trust in service leadership and empowerment is undeniably important. An empowered team feels more supported and has far greater capacity to care for the customer.

Empowerment and trust

It has been said the best way to make someone trustworthy is to trust them. Leaders who empower their employees are more likely to be trusted than leaders who do not.

In her book, *Dare to Lead*, professor and researcher Brené Brown writes that 'Trust is earned in the smallest of moments. It is earned not through heroic deeds, or even highly visible actions, but through paying attention, listening, and gestures of genuine care and connection'.[2]

Nordstrom is a luxury US department store chain founded in 1901. The company is world-famous for its customer experience and legendary service. It trusts team members from the moment they are hired. Among the paperwork given to team members on their first day of orientation is a 5½" x 7½" card titled 'Nordstrom Employee Handbook', which features one important line: 'Use good judgement in all situations.'

This simple six-word directive is the foundation upon which the Nordstrom Way is built. It illustrates the company's culture of empowering people and showing them they are trusted.

To counter any uncertainty, the statement is followed by, 'Please feel free to ask your manager or Human Resources any questions at any time'.

This rule simultaneously places enormous trust in the team and offers leadership support when required. Nordstrom is often held up as an example of exceptional customer experience driven by exceptional people who are trusted and empowered to do their job.[3]

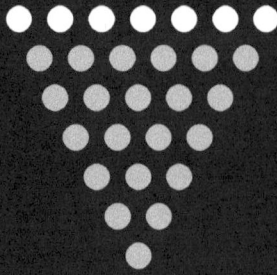

Chapter Summary

Practical tips

- At your next meeting, ask your team if they feel empowered to help customers. Encourage honesty and listen to their feedback.

- If the team members express that they don't feel empowered, probe further and ask why. Instigate any changes that need to be made.

- Examine discretionary spend limits to ensure they are adequate for the team.

Reflection questions

- As a leader, do you empower your team to make decisions in the best interests of the customer?

- How do you help your team to continue to increase their knowledge base?

- Do you need to be an advocate to instigate changes for increased levels of discretionary spend for your team?

Actions to take:

Chapter Thirteen

The Voice of the Team

*'Leaders who don't listen will
eventually be surrounded by people
who have nothing to say.'*

– Andy Stanley

In any service-driven culture, there will be a strong emphasis on the voice of the customer. Equally, there needs to be a focus on the voice of the team. One of the best ways a service leader can engage their team is by listening to them. Begin by asking your team how you can help them do their job better.

The voice of the team can be about improving the employee or customer experience, improving workplace culture, productivity and efficiency, or improving business processes and systems. The frontline team hears many first-hand customer frustrations, obstacles, pain points and direct feedback through their conversations and customer relationships. They hear when customers verbally express their frustration or ideas, 'If only I could...' or 'It would be easier if...' or 'It is so difficult when...'.

When the frontline hears this from the customer and knows their voice is valued and an integral part of their role, they will be far more alert and present to opportunities to capture customer feedback and insights. They will do so knowing that both their and the customers' voices matter equally to the organisation and leadership.

The team often has many brilliant ideas for improving the customer experience. Make 'employee listening' a cultural value and create a place of psychological safety where people know it is safe and are encouraged to speak up. Ideas may be generated in the moment, post-call or conversation, or after a team meeting. Capture these moments as they arise.

Professor of organisational behaviour at London Business School, Dan Cable, wrote, '...servant leaders have the humility, courage, and insight to admit that they can benefit from the expertise of others who have less power than them. They actively seek the ideas and unique contributions of the employees that they serve. This is how servant leaders create a culture of learning and an atmosphere that encourages followers to become the very best they can.'[4]

In the 2021 Qualtrics XM Employee Experience Trends Study, 92% of those surveyed believe it's important that their company listens to feedback. Yet only 7% say their company acts on feedback well.[5]

Listening to employee feedback and translating it into action has a direct, positive effect on the employee experience. As the number of employees who feel their company takes action on feedback increases, so does their intent to stay and their engagement. When employees feel a company acts well on feedback, their engagement is more than double that of workers who feel it's not acted on or acted on only slightly. Further data from the Qualtrics study shows that listening without taking action results in worse engagement than if you don't have a listening program at all.[6]

Over the years, I have seen the impact of leaders not listening to their people. The word that springs to mind is apathy. When people have tried to speak up and have their ideas heard, but no one listens, there comes a point when they stop trying. This shows up in my workshops when I ask for input and the response is, 'Why bother? No one is going to listen to us anyway'. From the team member's perspective, it feels like banging your head against a brick wall and getting nowhere.

The five steps of feedback

The five-step feedback model is a methodology you can use as a service leader to maximise input and engagement. It outlines each step from asking through to implementation. This should be a never-ending cycle of continuous improvement and a way to engage and recognise the team so the feedback keeps coming.

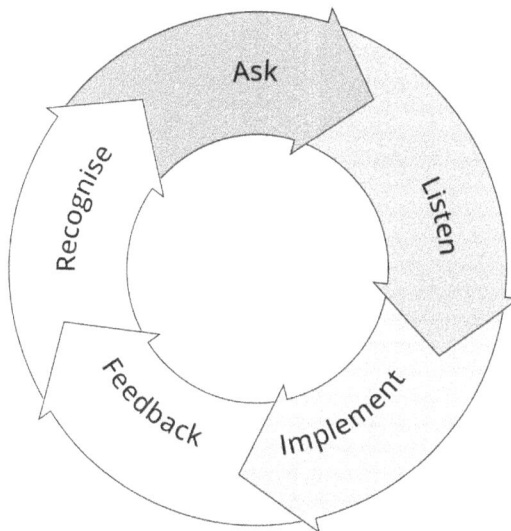

Figure 10: The five steps of feedback

Ask

Listening to feedback is integral, but having a structured avenue to collect it is even more important. This can include a range of methodologies, from formal surveys to ongoing in-the-moment channels. Why wait for the annual or bi-annual company survey to ask for feedback? It should be a constant part of every service leader's role alongside the formal capture.

Microsoft surveys more than 2,500 employees every day, but ensures people only get one survey per quarter. This data helps Dawn Klinghoffer, head of People Analytics, to immediately see signs of burnout, stress, work-life balance, and dozens of other issues. The company is constantly redesigning work practices from this data.[7]

The Hilton Hotel chain, another company that excels at employee and customer listening, also surveys their location employees daily. These quick surveys are analysed and compared with daily customer surveys so the team can immediately see if a location has issues. For example, if the cleaning team has problems with the equipment, they speak up. And sure enough, it has a direct impact on customer net promoter scores.[8]

Obtaining feedback can be as simple as asking in team meetings, informal catch-ups or one-on-ones. The message is simple. Ask!

Listen

Listening is one of the most important attributes of a service leader — listening to the words spoken and what is unsaid. Creating space to listen, encouraging everyone's ideas (not just the vocal team members) and providing time and space are crucial in gaining ideas and input.

Recently I worked with Bass Coast Shire Council in rural Victoria. The organisation is very customer-focused and proactively creates opportunities for customers and the team to share feedback. I worked with the business improvement team that instigated the training and then with each department on a customer journey mapping activity. Through this, each department came up with ideas and initiatives to improve the customer experience. This feedback was documented and is now being reviewed and implemented with the support of the business improvement team. They listen to what is said and go beyond to take action.

Feedback

A bi-annual or annual employee engagement survey is a significant opportunity to let the team know they have been heard. But don't just ask for feedback; share the results. That includes being honest, open and transparent and ensuring the feedback is shared across the organisation, then followed up with an action plan.

The best way to have team members respond flippantly or hit the delete button when the annual survey arrives is if you never share the results. The organisation risks employees not taking the survey seriously and becoming disengaged. The lack of a feedback loop triggers apathy and demotivation. Even if the ideas cannot be implemented, explaining why is crucial for ongoing engagement.

Whenever the issue of not receiving feedback has come up in my workshops with the frontline, I promised to write a book on service leadership and include a chapter on this very topic and the importance of what I refer to as 'feedback on feedback'. And here it is!

The team may come to you with ideas that cannot be implemented because of time, cost or resources. Respond anyway. Hearing nothing is demotivating. It's incredibly powerful when a leader takes time to speak with the team member or team about how much they appreciate and value the ideas and explains why their idea cannot be progressed. Closing the loop is a crucial component of building a listening culture.

Implement

Ideas without action are a waste. There are many ways to get moving without landing all the responsibility on the team leader. Creating working groups and giving the team time and space to work on improvement initiatives are all part of successful implementation. Quick wins are always inspiring, while others take time and form part of longer-term projects. Involve the team and give them autonomy and empowerment to implement the ideas. Be available as a listening ear.

Recognise

A further benefit of a well-designed team voice program is using it for recognition. Celebrating ideas from individuals or teams that have improved the customer or employee experience, productivity, or technology has a powerful impact on morale, motivation and continuing to give feedback.

When leaders don't listen

If people are not listened to, this can also impact attrition. One famous example is Eric Yuan, co-founder and CEO of Zoom Video Communications, who used to work with Cisco WebEx. As he expressed, he was embarrassed to learn that not a single user was happy with the Cisco service. He tried to rebuild the platform but could not convince his colleagues, and his feedback was ignored. That is when he decided to leave the company and start Zoom. His goal was simple, 'a better service bringing happiness back to these customers'. At the time of writing, Zoom is worth US$19.49 billion.

Leaders who listen

Leaders who listen have an immediate impact. When Chris Kempczinski took on the role of McDonald's CEO in 2018, he began reaching out to employees for feedback about the company. In an open invitation, Kempczinski asked employees to reflect on and share things they were proud of in their working life and what the CEO could do to make them prouder to work for the business.

David Abney was nineteen years old when he joined the shipping and logistics company UPS, loading packages onto vans at the local depot at night to make extra money while he was studying. Forty years later, Abney had risen through the ranks to become CEO of the company. He credits much of his success to listening intentionally to employees.

One of the first things Abney did upon being named CEO was to go on a worldwide listening tour. He invited the company's employees and customers to tell him what they thought the company should focus on going forward. One anonymous UPS employee shared, 'When David issued a call for ideas, many of which were actually implemented, it was almost earth-shattering. We couldn't believe leadership was finally listening and taking action on our recommendations.'[9]

The benefits of listening

Listening can also impact profitability and cost savings. The Audi ideas program resulted in US$133 million in savings in 2017 alone from listening to employees' ideas.

The benefits of the voice of the team include improved productivity, efficiency and profitability, as well as improved employee retention and engagement, improved job satisfaction and improved customer experience. Service leaders who listen show that they care.

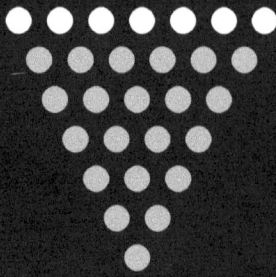

Chapter Summary

Practical tips

- Ensure there's a system in place for capturing the voice of the team.

- Share results of the formal employee engagement survey.

- Involve the team in continuous improvement and bringing their ideas to life. Give them space and time to create the required changes.

- Take time to recognise individual team members and the team for improvement ideas.

- Give 'feedback on feedback' by closing the feedback loop, even if ideas cannot be implemented for cost or resource reasons.

Reflection questions

- Does your organisation have a voice of the team program?

- As a leader, do you share the results of your employee engagement survey?

- How do you currently use recognition in conjunction with the voice of the team program?

Actions to take:

PART FOUR

EMBED

Chapter Fourteen

Service Coaching

'A good coach can change a game;
a great coach can change a life.'

– John Wooden

Coaching is one of the most vital skills that any service leader can master to develop each team member. It is about fostering a collaborative and empowering approach, directing people towards their own resourcefulness and insights and helping them to be the best they can be. Coaching is a critical leadership skill, and coaching customer-focused skills and behaviours is vital for long-term behavioural change.

Coaching supports ongoing team member development. It can also be used to improve performance and provides personal attention for the team member to address performance gaps with the aim of sustained behavioural change.

Leadership development specialists Zenger Folkman completed research based on 360° assessments of 25,000 leaders. They found that the top 10% of effective coaches had the top 10% of employee commitment. Employees who are coached regularly had three times the level of engagement. The research also found that effective coaching led to improved productivity or willingness to go the extra mile, fewer employees thinking about quitting, increased retention and commitment, and positive opinions about their leader.[1]

Benefits of coaching

Effective coaching offers benefits for the coachee, the organisation and the customer. It helps improve individual performance, take more responsibility and accountability and can create a fundamental shift in the approach to work. One study from the International Coaching Federation (ICF) found that coaching has a median company return of 700% and is often reported to impact employee morale and retention positively.[2]

All service leaders must also be committed service coaches and prioritise coaching within their day and week. Given that customer service is often such a busy, fast-paced environment, how we coach in a customer service environment may be slightly different from other corporate environments. Service coaching may also be referred to as on-the-job, corridor or in-the-moment coaching. But like any coaching, it is all about helping, supporting and sustaining performance.

Think of the coaches you may have had. Perhaps it was in the workplace, in a sports team, or you sing or play a musical instrument. A coach can have a major impact, and an extraordinary coach's influence is immeasurable.

Service coaching is a critical leadership skill that can be learned. Leaders must have the tools, mindset and training to be effective coaches. There is an art and a methodology to providing meaningful coaching and feedback that doesn't feel personal, is constructive and helps shift performance and improve the customer experience.

I recently spoke with a brilliant customer experience manager. He shared the story of one of his team leaders who had wonderful rapport and connection with her team yet found it incredibly difficult to deal with team members when they did not deliver the expected levels of customer service. The prospect filled her with dread, so she actively avoided such situations. That meant the behaviour continued and, in some cases, worsened.

In my experience of working with many leaders over the years, this problem occurs if the leader sees giving feedback as personal. Equally, if feedback is delivered in this way, there will be resistance from the team member. That is when clarity around service standards and behaviours is critical. When coaching conversations are needed about customer service performance, it always ties back to the documented and defined service standards and behaviours.

Service standards that are clearly identified, articulated and socialised within the organisation are the first step to successfully utilising service coaching as a way of embedding behaviours, improving performance and increasing engagement. If the team is clear about the expected standards and behaviours and is not meeting these, there is nothing personal about it. It is simply an identified opportunity to improve through a supportive conversation. This can be achieved through effective service coaching, which can be practised and improved.

One of the myths about service coaching is that it is time-consuming. I am very aware of the many demands on service leaders' time and resources. Coaching can be done quickly and effectively through positive intent and with tremendous impact.

What matters is how we conduct the coaching conversation. At the heart of all successful coaching is care and (most importantly) listening, not telling.

The Three Cs of Coaching

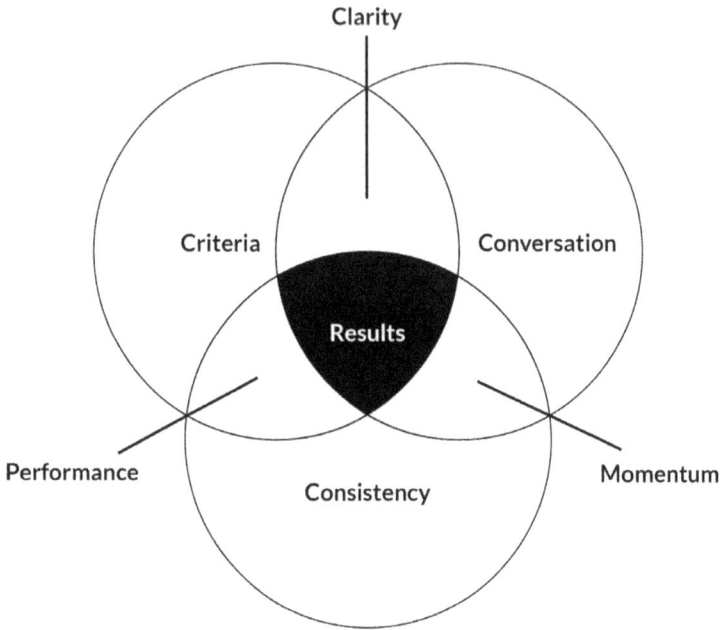

Figure 11: The three Cs of coaching

In service coaching, there are Three Cs, which refer to the criteria, consistency and the conversation.

Criteria

The team is coached on the service standards and associated behaviours. Make sure there are clearly defined expectations before you commence any coaching. The team needs to be fully aware of the service standards and have had training on them to ensure they are working towards logical goals. The criteria (service standards) will be different for each organisation.

Consistency

This refers to the frequency of the coaching, which can be ad-hoc, side-by-side in a physical environment, listening to a number of calls per team member each month in a contact centre, through to scheduled virtual coaching. The frequency is critical if we want to improve performance. Think about playing a sport or learning to sing; we don't do it once a year. We receive regular coaching to improve and sustain performance. It is a way of integrating learning and connection into the normal working environment.

Conversation

Most importantly, this is how we have the conversation in a way that builds connection and trust. Rapport-building, care and communication skills are at the heart of coaching conversations and are achieved through listening, focus and attention.

Service leaders must create a strong connection and an environment where the team member feels safe sharing what's going on for them.

The Service Coaching model

The Service Coaching model outlines the five steps in a coaching conversation.

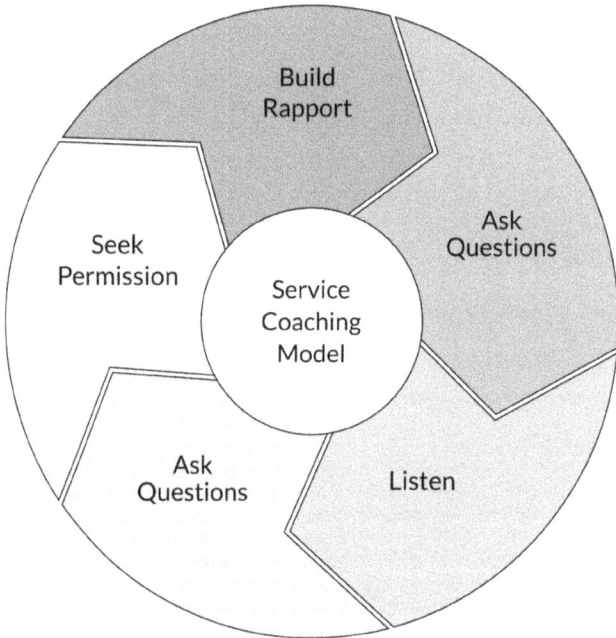

Figure 12: The five step service coaching model

Step 1: Build rapport

Building rapport is about making sure the coachee feels comfortable and safe. This can be achieved through brief social chat or simply asking them how their day is going. Rapport is connection, so establish it before a coaching conversation occurs. Service leaders likely already have strong relationships with each team member.

I recommend starting every coaching conversation with a check-in to ensure there are no external factors contributing to performance. This could be as simple as 'Tell me about your day' or 'How are you finding work at the moment?' Simple rapport-building questions that aim to build connection and open up a conversation.

I once asked an initial check-in question with a new team member who was not delivering the expected level of customer service, only to find out she was going through a very messy separation. After learning this, the direction of the coaching session and conversation changed completely and became about the support and care we could offer her.

Once rapport is built and the coachee feels comfortable and open, the coaching conversation can begin.

Step 2: Ask questions

The foundation of service coaching is asking, not telling. Your role is to ask open questions, reflect and listen to the response. While it may be perceived as quicker and easier to tell, it doesn't have the same impact because there is no opportunity for the team member to reflect on their behaviour.

I once coached a very self-aware service leader. As soon as we explored the difference between asking and telling, he exclaimed, 'Yes! That is exactly what I do. I just tell. I don't ask questions!' After we had been through the service coaching model, he could see why asking questions is so powerful. He took that skill into future coaching conversations, which made all the difference to the connection and performance of his team.

Perhaps you have observed a team member who got a bit overheated in a conversation with a customer. You have been sitting nearby and heard them raise their voice and use a lot of negative language. The conversation obviously hasn't gone well. This could be a perfect opportunity for service coaching.

When the time is right, have a chat with the team member. After building rapport, start with simple, open questions such as 'How are you going? Is everything OK?' You may continue with 'How do you feel that call went? It sounded like it might have been a really difficult one.' Asking those questions shows empathy and care and invites the team member to share feedback about the call.

Step 3: Listen

The most important coaching skill is the ability to listen actively. This is about being present, focusing on the other person and what they are saying and ensuring you don't interrupt. Active listening includes appropriate eye contact, open body language and showing interest in the other person. If they feel we are truly listening, they will be more willing to open up and share.

Step 4: Ask questions

The team member may respond with something like, 'Well, actually, I found that a really hard call. I think I lost it a bit with the customer and got a bit angry'. Acknowledging their honesty and self-awareness before asking your next question. 'Thank you for being so honest, so what did you find difficult about that call?'

Ask a question, listen, reflect, ask a question. Repeat.

Note that they may also need time to cool down after a conversation that went wrong. After all, we can be embarrassed when caught out with poor behaviour. They may also need an opportunity to vent their frustration. Your coachee might respond, 'Well, the customer was rude and obnoxious', and take no responsibility for their part in the escalation. If this occurs, use the opportunity to coach around mindset. Remind them that while they cannot control how the customer behaves, they can always control how they choose to respond.

This process continues until you get all the information you need. At that point, one of my favourite coaching questions is: 'So what is it that you would do differently next time?' or 'If you had that call again, what strategies would you use?'

Give the coachee space to reflect on their behaviour and come up with a response. For example, they may say, 'Well, if I had stopped, and if I had done my breathing as we talked about in training, and if I had just remained calm, it would have been a completely different conversation'. They may end up sharing feedback that you would have given them, but when it comes from a place of self-reflection, it has far more power to shift behaviours.

Step 5: Seek permission

When the team member shares everything you might have told them, thank them for their time and let them know you're always available if they have any questions. Set a time to follow up and see how they are going. This is critical in offering ongoing support so the coachee knows you are there should they need you.

Have you ever met someone who gives you unsolicited advice or feedback? It can be annoying and frustrating. If you would like to share additional information, always seek permission. I never give feedback unless I ask the coachee's permission first.

This might be phrased as, 'Do you mind if I give you some feedback?' or 'Are you happy for me to share some things that I found really useful when I was on the phones?'

Pause and wait for the team member to respond. As a service leader, you have experience, insights and valuable information that can extend their thinking and learning and help them develop further. It is a golden opportunity for the coachee to learn from you. People are far more accepting of advice when they invite feedback.

This concludes your coaching conversation, which, in many cases, might have taken a matter of minutes. It can be done after hearing a call, after an observation that you've had with a customer service interaction, if you are working alongside the team member or after an email you have just read. Of course, timing is everything. Make sure it is the right time and consider who else is within hearing so it's a comfortable environment for a coaching conversation.

It is also worthwhile committing to an informal follow-up conversation or check in to ensure the team member has been able to apply their reflections and learnings. Make a note of the conversation for future reference.

What does a 'telling' conversation look like?

People don't learn from 'telling' conversations. They can be resistant and unreceptive to feedback. In the example above, a telling conversation might be: 'I just heard you speaking with the customer, and you raised your voice. I could tell the conversation was getting really heated, and that is not what we stand for here. Please make sure next time you stay calm and don't speak to the customer in that manner.'

Quick? Yes. Effective, No.

There is no learning in this conversation. If anything, it does more harm than good and can result in the team member getting offside, defensive and disengaged. As a service leader, avoid getting into telling mode at all costs! The only time I would ever recommend a leader go into 'telling' mode is if there is an immediate safety risk.

How to manage an unreceptive coachee

The more questions you ask, the more likely you will open up dialogue. However, there may be an instance with service coaching where you have an unreceptive coachee. You may attempt to build rapport and open with the question, 'How are you going? Is everything OK?' And you are met with 'Fine'. You attempt to probe further and ask. 'How do you feel you went with that call?' and get a stonewalled response, such as 'Fine'. So, you follow up with, 'What did you find most difficult?' And receive 'Nothing'.

While this rarely happens, we need to be more direct if the team member is unwilling to engage. That might involve language such as, 'I observed with that call that you raised your voice and appeared to get quite frustrated with the customer. Why were you frustrated?' We are still trying to open up the conversation.

If they are still unwilling, then after attempting to ask questions, use more direct language such as 'What I would suggest' or 'What I would recommend in future' or 'What I would do differently next time'. This enables you to give feedback and address behaviours that are not in line with the culture you are trying to create. If they are really blocking you, your last resort is to say, 'As you know, our customer experience is critical and I have identified some opportunities for improvement'.

While you won't see this often, it is a reminder that we can still have behaviours that are not in line with the service culture you are trying to create. The conversation needs to take place — even with an unreceptive coachee.

Remote service coaching

As workplaces have changed to include global teams, working virtually from home and in hybrid models, service coaching will not always be conducted in person. Remote coaching can be via phone or video through the organisation's preferred technology platform. Email can be helpful for follow-up questions and other resources, but it's much less useful for in-the-moment coaching. Texts can be ideal for quick messages but less impactful for coaching.

Being able to focus without interruption or technology failures and allowing adequate time is important in remote coaching. Consider background noise, eliminating interruptions, sending emails and working on other tasks. If the coachee feels you are not present or listening, they will likely shut down. The five step model can be used in virtual coaching, as trust and connection remain important.

The cycle of service coaching becomes part of our culture and the 'way we do things around here'. It is such a valuable tool to build connection and rapport and to continue to embed the behaviours we wish to see. The team looks forward to it as a positive learning and growth opportunity. Leaders who have embraced a coaching philosophy feel more confident in providing feedback. They get results.

Exceptional service leaders are also exceptional coaches, and the role of any leader is to focus on helping each team member be the best they can be. Effective service coaching removes any personal element and provides a platform for open discussion, exploration and willingness to listen and improve. All of which ultimately create positive employee and customer experiences.

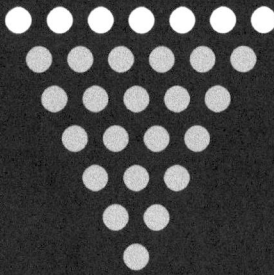

Chapter Summary

Practical tips

- Ensure the team is aware and fully trained in the service standards. Be very specific about the service behaviours you are coaching.

- Find opportunities to provide coaching moments with your team. This can be done remotely or in person. Be creative! You can coach on the job, out on the road, or side-by-side while listening to calls.

- Remember, at the heart of coaching is asking insightful questions, listening, and further probing with more questions. Avoid shifting into 'telling' mode at all costs. While it might be quicker, it does not have the same impact on the person or the behaviour.

- Balance coaching with recognition. An individual or team that is regularly recognised will be far more receptive to coaching.

- With remote coaching, ensure you have an optimum environment to minimise distractions and enable you to focus.

Reflection questions

- What defined criteria do you use to provide coaching?

- How often do you coach your team?

- What methodologies are you using? (Planned, coaching in the moment, side-by-side, silent monitoring)

- Are you more likely to ask questions or shift into 'telling' mode?

- How could you incorporate more service coaching into your daily work?

Actions to take:

Chapter Fifteen

The Art of Recognition

'Appreciation can make a day, even change a life. Your willingness to put it into words is all that is necessary.'

– Margaret Cousins

Every human needs to feel appreciated. While customer service professionals have told me many things, I've never heard, 'We get too much recognition and appreciation. Our leaders just need to stop!' Letting team members know their work is appreciated is a critical leadership skill.

In fact, what I hear more than anything is just how de-motivating the lack of recognition can be. According to Gallup's research, 'Lack of recognition is a significant reason why employees leave their jobs, and 'the more talented the employee is, the faster they leave'.[3]

Recognition is a service leadership habit. If you set a standard of regular recognition, it will quickly become a part of the team culture. Service leaders are intentional in how they take the time to recognise their team's efforts. It is also important to note the difference between reward, recognition and appreciation.

A reward is a tangible acknowledgement of accomplishments. Gifts and awards are common examples of rewards employees may receive. Recognition can happen anytime someone notices positive behaviours and includes recognition of milestones, performance and results.

Reward	Recognition
Planned	Can be in the moment of planned
Transactional	Relational
Tied to goals and accomplishment	Tied to specific behaviours
Often economical	Usually free
Tangible	Intangible

Figure 13: The difference between reward and recognition

It is also worth noting the impact of appreciation. While sitting outside reward and recognition, appreciation is about acknowledging a person's inherent value. The point isn't their accomplishments; it's their worth as a colleague and a person. In simple terms, recognition is about what people do; appreciation is about who they are.[4] I love the concept of appreciation, as it isn't tied to anything. It is simply about a leader appreciating each team member for who they are and what they bring to the team. Everyone needs that.

The benefits of recognition

The benefits of recognition are many. When team members are recognised, motivation increases, engagement increases and the behaviours you acknowledge are more likely to continue. It also increases retention and company loyalty and improves productivity and morale. Deloitte found that organisations with recognition programs had 31% lower voluntary turnover than those without. Employee engagement, productivity, and performance were 14% higher than in organisations without recognition.[5]

It is essential to map out the behaviours and actions you are looking for, tie them to your service standards and customer experience and ensure everyone in the team has an equal opportunity to be recognised.

Every team member is different and will be motivated by different things. Get to know your team members as individuals, discover what motivates them, and find a good mixture of extrinsic and intrinsic motivators, so you can encourage them to create valuable customer experiences.

The three-step recognition process

Meaningful recognition by a service leader can be achieved in three simple steps.

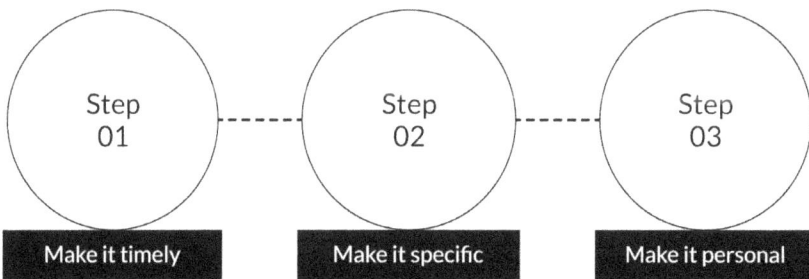

Step
01

Step
02

Step
03

Make it timely

Make it specific

Make it personal

Figure 14: The three-step recognition process

Make it timely

Recognition should occur as close to the event as possible. This has far more impact than saving it up to share during an annual review. It will also be more front of mind with the team member, which helps with meaning and relevance. If left too long, people forget, and the context can be lost.

Timely recognition also lets the team member know the positive impact, and they will be more willing and able to repeat desired behaviours and actions more frequently.

Meaningful feedback and recognition along the way are essential in long-term projects. Celebrating milestones impacts motivation.

Be specific

Be specific about the behaviour you are recognising. This is particularly important when recognising service standards and behaviours you wish to continue or have been working on with a team member during coaching. Consider the following examples. Which do you think has more impact when delivered by a leader?

'Well done, that was excellent.'

Or

'Well done, that was excellent. I loved how you acknowledged the customer when they came into the store and introduced yourself before offering help. What great personalised service!'

The second example has more impact, meaning the likelihood of the behaviour occurring again is much higher.

Highlight the behaviour you wish to see more of.

Make it personalised

One of the most important parts of the recognition process is ensuring that it is personalised and tailored to the individual and how they like to be recognised. To make recognition meaningful, learn how each person in your team is uniquely motivated.

In a former role, I was the training manager in a contact centre, and one of the ways that the team was recognised for exemplary customer service was through tickets to the Australian Grand Prix. Two team members were the recipients of the award. Susie was a car enthusiast and Holden was her favourite team. She lived for car racing and often wore her Holden jacket to work. The other team member, Megumi, wasn't fond of car racing. She had a young child and had zero interest in the Grand Prix. Yet they received the same recognition for the level of customer service they had achieved. This illustrates how the same reward had significantly different meaning and impact for two very different people.

To personalise recognition, you have to get to know your team. Know what makes each person tick. What is important to them? What are their preferences? Do they eat chocolate? Are they gluten-free? Are they parents or carers who would prefer an afternoon off so that they can go to their child's school concert? A bottle of wine means nothing to somebody who doesn't drink alcohol. A wrong gift can be worse than nothing at all!

The more we get to know our teams, the more we can personalise their recognition. I call it my game of 'secret squirrel' to find out what people love and make recognition and gratitude meaningful. Pay attention to what each team member says when they share their likes, interests and preferences. Remember and make a note of it. It will make an enormous difference to your recognition efforts.

I am often asked whether recognition should be done in public or private. Once again, this comes down to knowing the person's individual preferences.

Some people in your team will prefer recognition to be directly delivered by you and shun the limelight. Other team members love public recognition and applause in front of an audience. Sharing what they're doing in front of other people motivates them even further. This type of recognition can backfire if somebody doesn't like public recognition.

I once worked with a team member who was an exceptional performer, delivered extraordinary customer service and had the best statistics in the team. As a result, they kept winning the team member of the month. The award was handed out in person, in front of everyone, and they hated it. The upshot was that it had the reverse impact, and they intentionally started underperforming, so they didn't have to be recognised publicly. Our genuine efforts can be undone if we don't know our team members and what they prefer.

Make sure that recognition is genuine, sincere and from the heart. People can smell feigned recognition a mile off.

Who do we recognise?

While recognition can be individual, it can also be to the entire team. It may be that the team has worked incredibly hard to get customer requests down, or they've worked extra hours because there were so many enquiries. 'Managers also need to tread carefully when recognizing everyone on a team. Sometimes a group's performance is not a reflection of equal contributions from all its members, and you run the risk of alienating high performers if everyone receives the same recognition.'[6]

As leaders, fostering recognition within the team and looking for ways to encourage peer-to-peer recognition are equally important. Look for opportunities for internal departmental recognition, as another team may have helped the customer service team create a positive customer experience. Providing internal recognition can make a huge difference to the support team. This is particularly so if an organisation is trying to build a service culture.

There are many different ways to recognise other people and departments. An IT team I worked with had one customer for whom they had gone above and beyond to rectify an urgent problem. The internal customer brought a lovingly homemade chocolate cake to thank the team for their help with an on-air issue. It truly made their day.

Get creative! A recognition menu

There are countless ways to recognise the team. Many are low-cost and high-impact. Have fun with your recognition ideas.

I think of recognition as a menu; it is about choosing the right thing for the right person. With changes to how we work, including working from home and hybrid models, it is essential to tailor recognition efforts to all team members, so don't forget those working remotely. Here are some practical ideas to incorporate into your daily work:

Say thank you – in person or with a handwritten card or note

Never underestimate the power of a sincere thank you. Deloitte studied 'The Practical Magic of Thank You' with 16,000 people from more than 100 countries. For day-to-day efforts, 85% of people wanted to hear 'Thank you', with 54% preferring verbal appreciation and 31% via a note.[7] It is so important that leaders take time to acknowledge and recognise the team. I recommend that every service leader keeps a pack of thank-you cards ready to use at any moment. A handwritten card or note can have real impact, particularly in the digital age.

Celebrate customer service results

This could be recognising improvements in customer satisfaction ratings, improved net promoter or customer effort scores. One client held an end-of-year party for all team members and leaders once they achieved their customer satisfaction target. The team loved this, as they highly valued socialising together. You might recognise the number of requests down or customer emails responded to. Finding a way to tie recognition with customer service efforts can make a big difference, particularly when focusing on strengthening or shifting a service culture.

Online recognition

Organisations, teams and leaders increasingly use technology to power their recognition programs by integrating recognition into their culture. These include tools such as Slack, MS Teams, internal intranets and apps.

Senior leadership recognition

I began my career in hospitality at The Keg restaurant chain, which was incredibly guest-focused. It's where I learnt so much of my service ethos. I still remember the letter I received from our director of operations, Peter Laurie, thanking me for the compliment letter a guest had written about me and my service.

Forwarding a customer compliment and having a senior leader reach out with congratulations is a low-cost way to provide meaningful recognition.

Celebrate milestones

Christopher Littlefield is an international speaker and expert in employee appreciation and my friend and colleague. During one of his workshops, he said, 'We don't give someone a birthday card or gift every five or twenty years, so why do we do this with recognition instead of every single day and every single year?' This really stuck with me as so many organisations focus on five- or ten-year recognition efforts.

Every manager should have each team member's work anniversary in their calendar and recognise it each year, just as you would a birthday or anniversary. I know leaders who tie balloons to the team member's chair on their work anniversary or take the person out to lunch. Years of service should be celebrated every year — just like birthdays!

One of my favourite examples of acknowledging longevity of service is the supermarket chain Coles, which celebrates and honours its most experienced team members with loyal service luncheons across the country. More than four thousand team members have over twenty-five years of service across the brands and supply chain. Coles uses this as an opportunity to celebrate the contribution of all long-term team members.

Formal recognition and awards

Formal recognition programs require more structure, communication, criteria and fairness than informal methods. These can include monthly awards, customer service team member or customer service team of the year. It may also be appropriate to nominate the team for external industry awards in service. When done well, these can be incredibly motivating and an opportunity to share successes with the team, organisation and customers.

Development opportunities

Attending a conference, participating in a training program or working on a special project can be another way to recognise a team member. This has the bonus of impacting skills development. Having a team member with leadership aspirations take on an acting team leader role can be fantastic recognition for the right person. It can, of course, have a reverse impact on someone without those aspirations. Align the development opportunity with the team member.

Volunteering and donations

More than ever, team members appreciate purpose and having time off to volunteer. Supporting a charity through a donation can be another way to recognise the team. It may be a charity the organisation supports or one that is dear to the team member. Donations of time and money can be very powerful.

Food

While food is one of my favourite things, I mention it here because so many team members have shared that they appreciate a thank you morning tea, doughnuts, pizza or chocolates. Make sure you know team member preferences; for example, ensure there is halal or gluten-free food for those who need it. This shows additional care and consideration.

While in high school, I worked part-time at my local supermarket and learned the power of recognition. Our delicatessen manager was very stressed because sales were down and she had a mountain of excess stock. I offered to come in on the weekend when I wasn't working and cook chicken skewers on a grill at the front of the store. I sold a massive number of chicken skewers, had a fabulous day and the customers were all very happy.

The following Thursday, I was working away and heard a call over the PA system, 'Monique Richardson, can you please come to the manager's office?' With great fear and trepidation, I walked up the wooden stairs, wondering why on earth I was being called in.

The store manager, Andrew, asked me to sit down and started chatting. Then he said, 'It has been bought to my attention that you came in on the weekend when you weren't rostered, to cook chicken skewers to help the deli. Is that correct?' 'Yes', I answered sheepishly, then started frantically thinking, 'Have I broken a rule? Have I done something wrong? Why on earth did I do that?' Andrew pulled two huge boxes of chocolates from under his desk and said, 'I just wanted to say thank you for what you did to help. It means a lot.'

It wasn't about the chocolates because as much as I love and appreciate them, there was a whole range in aisle nine he could have chosen from. What was most powerful was that at the age of 15, I learned that day that extra effort mattered. I carried this single act of recognition by leadership into every future job. Not for the reward, but for knowing that my efforts were appreciated and had made a difference. It shifted the way I saw my work and approached every role after that.

One of a service leader's most important responsibilities is to show care and gratitude and find ways to let the team know how much they are appreciated. In the words of Bruce Jones, senior programming director at the Disney Institute, '(Here), we teach business leaders that they must proactively search for and recognize employees who demonstrate their organization's desired behaviors'. In other words, they need to find people who are doing 'it' right.

It is a little thing that makes a big difference!

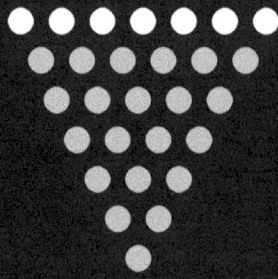

Chapter Summary

Practical tips

- Note your team's preferences, hobbies and tastes, so you know what will create the most meaningful recognition for them.

- Have a box of thank-you cards ready at your desk. Make time to send a handwritten card or note.

- Have a conversation with each team member when they first join. Ask them, 'How do you like to be recognised? Publicly? In private? What recognition has the biggest impact on you?'

- Put all team member birthdays and work anniversaries into your calendar and create meaningful acknowledgements.

- Find ways to recognise individual team members, the team and other departments within your organisation.

Reflection questions

- When did you last recognise one of your team? How often do you do so? Is it frequent enough?

- Who could you recognise individually in your team? How could you recognise the entire team?

- How does each member of your team prefer to be recognised?

- What customer success stories or positive customer feedback could you share with your team?

- Is there another team within the organisation that has supported you in service delivery? How could you let them know how they made a difference?

Actions to take:

Chapter Sixteen

Reinforcing and Sustaining Success

*'Enthusiasm...the sustaining
power of all great action.'*

– Samuel Smiles

Have you ever had a burst of motivation to get fit, purchased a gym membership, new workout gear and a shiny new water bottle, only to start and then stop? If so, you are not alone.

USA Today reports that 67% of gym memberships go completely unused. But even among those who do use their gym membership, many are not exactly regular. Finder.com says 56.6% of members use the gym twice a week, 20.7% go once a week, 6% go once a month, and 7.4% go less than once a month.[8]

Why is this?

It can be easy to start something, but maintaining it is a far bigger challenge. You only get results with sustained effort. You can't expect to go to the gym once and get fit. It is the same for customer service. It is not a one-off training event or something mentioned in the corporate orientation and never heard of again. Matt Church, one of my favourite mentors, says, 'It is the role of the leader to light the fire every day'.

Reinforce the behaviour you want more of

Reinforcing the importance of the customer is essential. The human brain stores information so that frequent use and repetition make it easily accessible. Sporadic use causes the information to slip further down our memories and be forgotten. It's like when you meet someone and learn their name. Chances are that if you see them often, you will remember their name. But if it is a year down the track and you haven't seen them, you're more likely to forget. Not because you have a bad memory; but because it is information you have not needed or accessed.

Behaviour increases in probability when its outcomes are reinforced. There are many theories of reinforcement in the field of psychology. One of the most regularly referenced is the theory and research of American psychologist B.F. Skinner, which asserts that you can alter someone's behaviour by rewarding good behaviour and discouraging bad behaviour. Punishments stop the behaviour you do not want, whereas rewards reinforce desired behaviour.

A fundamental idea in Skinner's theory is positive reinforcement, which refers to introducing a pleasurable or desired stimulus following a behaviour. Examples of this can be appreciation, a promotion, or any other reward that increases the possibility of the behaviours being repeated. This can also be applied to reinforce or teach new habits.

According to Skinner, learning is a proactive activity. Consequences result from human behaviour when it affects or changes their environment.

People continue acting in particular ways when the results are favourable and stop when the results are not. This does not account for the intrinsic motivations of each individual.

There are two main types of motivation — extrinsic and intrinsic. Extrinsic motivation is when you use external factors to encourage your team. This could include bonuses, positive feedback and reinforcement. Intrinsic motivation is internal. It is about a personal desire to overcome a challenge, produce high-quality work, or interact with team members you like and trust. Intrinsically motivated people get tremendous satisfaction and enjoyment from what they do.

Sustaining long-term success

Organisations that demonstrate a long-term commitment to building a service culture and reinforcing customer service principles reap the highest rewards.

I have had the privilege of working with the Melbourne Cricket Club (MCC) over the past six years. In 2015 the club recognised it needed to focus on improving the customer experience, so it introduced a program driven by one of the club's five strategic pillars (to improve customer satisfaction). The program was fully supported and endorsed by the board and the executive.

The principles and service standards came from input from team members, leaders and customers after they were asked what was most important regarding customer service at the 'G'. With the leaders' full support, I started by working a few shifts to truly understand the culture and what it was like to work on event days.

The program started with a town hall attended by board members, directors, leaders and all team members, where the CEO spoke and introduced the strategy and the CARE program. The first step was a program that ensured a leadership-driven approach to building a service culture. The training focused on coaching and embedding desired behaviours, recognition and sustaining a service culture. The 'CARE Squad' was introduced as a roving team that could proactively help customers.

We rolled the training out to 1,200 team members, all the game day team members and the support office team, including People and Culture, IT and finance. The program was then extended to partners of the MCG.

Since then, further training and CARE Plus have been delivered to all team members and now form part of every new team member induction. It is part of the orientation for all game-day, permanent team members, leaders and the executive.

I have never witnessed an organisation as committed to service as the MCC. So much supports the training internally, from weekly CARE messages, prizes, awards and celebrations. It is part of the organisation's DNA, embedded in the culture. That is why MCC is considered an industry leader. They have seen customer satisfaction ratings continue to rise and records broken because of their long-term commitment to improving the customer experience. This undertaking is led by an extraordinary senior leadership team that cares deeply about its people and its customers.

I'm always impressed by the number of team members who approach me during the orientation training to talk about the leadership. They describe what an incredible onboarding experience they have had and how much they feel cared for.

A long-term commitment to service builds results and a world-class service culture.

How to reinforce service

There are many ways to keep reinforcing knowledge shared during training and orientation. Creating a service culture is a long-term commitment driven by caring and focused service leaders. Try these practical ideas to keep customer service alive.

Start all meetings with a customer focus

Start every single meeting in every department with a message of customer focus. It could be about improved results, team wins, positive customer feedback, or a service challenge. However you do it, making customer service the number one agenda item at every meeting across an organisation sends a compelling message.

CEO forum

Creating world-class customer experiences starts with a customer-driven CEO. Having the CEO regularly reinforce the core messages via a townhall (virtual or in person), video messages or a newsletter is an excellent way to show senior leadership support and demonstrate the importance of the customer.

Celebrate wins and successes

Celebrate team or individual wins and successes and tie them back to efforts. For example, one council I worked with had a higher-than-desired number of outstanding customer requests. They shared this with the leadership and the team, and with a continued focus on reducing these and celebrating the wins along the way, they managed to get outstanding customer requests down to zero. I was very excited to receive a text message from the leadership team telling me of their success!

Celebrating can include sharing customer feedback, improved satisfaction results and increased net promoter scores. Shout the wins from the rooftops so everyone can hear them.

Focus on visual artefacts

Visual reminders are important — from screensavers and mouse pads to recognition walls filled with customer compliments, scores and service standards posters. Keep these fresh and updated; nothing is worse than faded, tattered posters or old results from 2015. Visual collaterals keep messages alive.

Utilise video

With the increasing use and impact of video, try some of these ideas. A monthly recording from the CEO. Short videos on a topic or a customer from each department on rotation. Share an inspiring TED talk or video on a service topic. Create a TikTok video with a quick clip or even a message from a customer. Get creative with video — any smartphone will do as the message is more important than the camera quality.

Share stories

Storytelling is incredibly powerful, from customer stories to team members or leadership stories. It is an art that can be learned and incorporated into videos, newsletters, a company e-book or shared in meetings. In the words of Gabrielle Dolan, global thought leader on strategic storytelling, 'Facts inform us and stories influence us'.

Include customer service in everyone's position description

Whether in a customer, non-customer facing or leadership role, customer service must be in everyone's position description. Its absence sends a message that it doesn't matter. From an employee perspective, why bother focusing on something that is not expected? Make it clear from the outset, then refer to it in ongoing catchups and reviews.

Use metrics that matter

The expression 'That which is not measured does not get done' rings true here. Clear goals must also be part of team goals. If there are no metrics around customer service performance for customer roles, non-customer facing or leadership roles, it will not be considered important.

Provide ongoing training

Ongoing training with embedding strategies is crucial for long-term behavioural change. The most successful organisations I work with have an annual focus on customer service training to keep the message alive and to continue to upskill the team. The content changes each time and is part of the ongoing development for each team member. Once again, this training must extend to customer and non-customer facing team members.

Share financial success

While this can vary depending on whether you're in the commercial or government sector, bonuses related to customer service results send a very powerful message. They reward performance and ensure everyone knows their role matters. Organisations such as Herman Miller have profit-sharing and employee-owned businesses.[9] Financial recognition is another way to increase buy-in for customer results and motivate everyone to focus on the customer.

Incorporate customer service training into orientation

Every new employee needs to be introduced to the service mindset and culture of the organisation. Do this as close to the start of employment as possible. I appreciate this may be difficult, as sometimes orientation is delayed until there are enough people to conduct a formal program. I recommend each leader creates a simple orientation focused on the customer for each team member on their first day.

The Greek philosopher Aristotle wrote, 'Virtues are formed in man by his doing the actions'. The writer Will Durant interpreted this as 'We are what we repeatedly do... therefore excellence is not an act, but a habit'. In other words: Excellence isn't this thing you do one time. It's a way of living. It's foundational.[10]

And that is the core message in reinforcing and sustaining a service mindset and culture; it is an ongoing and constant focus every day.

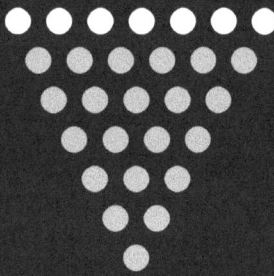

Chapter Summary

Practical tips

- Use recognition as a positive way to reinforce service.

- Make customer service the number one agenda item at every team meeting.

- Ensure each person who joins the organisation has customer service training. Provide ongoing refresher training.

- Incorporate customer-driven metrics to measure outcomes for all teams.

- Celebrate wins and success with each individual and the team.

Reflection questions

- How does your organisation reinforce the importance of customer service?

- What are you doing as a leader to reinforce the importance of customer service every day with your team?

- How could you improve the way customer service is reinforced?

Actions to take:

Chapter Seventeen

Supporting Your Team Through Change

'You must be the change you wish to see in the world.'

– Mahatma Gandhi

The magnitude of change required is determined by the gap between where your team's customer focus is now and where it needs to be.

I find it inspiring to work with clients who, despite exceptional success and customer feedback, still want to improve. It demonstrates a relentless pursuit of excellence.

For example, I worked on a service leadership program with the leadership team from Radiology Tasmania, which is owned by Capitol Health that has a net promoter score (NPS) of 90 plus. The creators of NPS, Bain & Company, suggest a score above 80 is world-class. Qualtrics XM describes a score of 100 as almost impossible to achieve. [11] So you can see how good this team is in terms of industry benchmarking. Yet, the leadership team still wanted to learn, improve and continue to serve their team in the best way possible.

I have always maintained it doesn't matter where you begin on a service cultural change journey; it is where you end up that matters. I have worked with organisations with poor service and customer satisfaction ratings that now rate among the best of the best. Anything is possible when you focus on service leadership, effort, persistence and team engagement.

Support from the CEO and executive leadership is pivotal in driving a customer-focused transformation. Every successful cultural change project I have ever been involved with has had the CEO and executive championing, supporting and driving the change.

People are fascinating, and they all respond differently to change. Have you ever noticed that some people are excited and love change while others resist it? Some people prefer stability and are motivated by a dependable, organised environment. There is no right or wrong, and leaders need to focus on accepting differences and helping to support people through change.

Why people resist change

As you work to develop a strong customer-focused culture and improve ways of working, you and your team may experience a range of emotions. King Whitney Jr is a change expert who expressed this beautifully when he wrote, 'Change can have a considerable psychological impact on the human mind. To the fearful, it is threatening because it means things may get worse. To the hopeful, it is encouraging because things may get better, and to the confident, it is inspiring because the challenge exists to make things better.'

People resist change for many reasons.

They don't understand the purpose

People need to understand the purpose of the change and why it is important to the organisation. This includes the vision and the rationale for the change and why it's essential. Having the background and reason for a decision helps the team to see the big picture and their role, which is essential for buy-in and understanding.

They don't understand how it will benefit them

I learnt many years ago about the concept of WIIFM — 'what's in it for me?' Leaders help people see how they will benefit from potential changes. Focusing on service makes customers' and team members' lives easier and happier. Show the team the benefits ahead, including short- and long-term gains.

They expect change to be difficult

Think about the last time you had to learn something new. Change can be hard, whether you're developing a new skill or starting a hobby. That is why I encourage all service leaders to regularly put themselves in the shoes of a learner. It is a valuable lesson in empathy and a reminder of how hard it can be.

I have recently started to learn how to play golf. As someone who has never picked up a golf club, it was daunting and felt strange and unfamiliar. Having an inspiring leader has made all the difference in persisting with something that felt so strange to start with. In my case, it's my coach Michael Sund, who demonstrates excellent coaching, patience, positivity and encouragement.

They are fearful

Our fears can be imagined or real; whether about loss, failure or new technology, they still loom large and create resistance to change. As workplace automation increases, fears grow that jobs will disappear as machines replace people. These may arise from experience, rumours or deep-seated worries about the impact of change.

They are cynical

Cynicism arises when prior attempts at change have failed or the organisation started on a customer service transformation and did not follow through. I commonly hear comments such as 'Here we go again' or 'We tried that before and it didn't work'. If you look through the eyes of the team member, it's easy to see why they might be cynical about change, particularly if they have witnessed stops, starts and big announcements that came to nothing.

They think everything is fine as it is

This can be one of the most challenging situations leaders face. I refer to it as the 'halo' effect. People think they are delivering great service, but customer feedback suggests otherwise. Statistics and real feedback can help the team see what customers are saying about the level of service offered. It paints a realistic picture of areas for improvement in a caring and empathetic manner.

How to engage the team to create a customer-focused culture

Now that we know why a customer-focused culture matters and the resistance you might face, let's look at tips for supporting and sustaining cultural change.

Validate

There is nothing more validating for a team member than when the leader acknowledges that change can be hard. Taking a cheerleader approach and telling people that the change will be positive can alienate those struggling with it and make them think there is something wrong with them. Keeping it real and meeting people where they are, makes them more likely to come on board when they are ready.

Engage

Involving your team members in your efforts to change the culture is one of the leader's most effective and powerful tools. Ask people for their ideas and use their input wherever possible throughout the change. The best ideas come from this opportunity to engage the team.

Keep the change alive

Emphasise the beliefs and principles of your organisation's service strategy, mission and vision with every new team member. Provide ongoing training, coaching and support and keep the subject of customer experience prominent in all communication. Many change efforts fail due to a lack of communication and reinforcement.

Change is not always easy, but it can bring rewards. One of the best work programs I was ever involved in was in the security industry. The organisation identified the need to shift from the traditional view of a guard to a more customer-focused approach. It was a significant change in mindset, skills and behaviours.

I believe security work is critical. It requires a focus on protecting people and assets as well as providing exceptional customer service. For this large team, it was a new way of thinking. There was initial resistance when I first arrived, as team members expressed frustration and concern that customer service would compromise security. They didn't want to be seen as 'soft' or possibly be taken advantage of. Rather than a quick session or one-off workshop, I delivered an intensive, tailored and focused program with follow-up and embedding tools. Listening to the team and validating their concerns was important in gaining their trust.

One way to promote change and shift service culture is by building pride in team roles. I asked the team to share examples of what made them proud. One of the guards spoke of protecting the prime minister and telling their family about it after their shift. Another described supporting a mother in delivering her baby in a hospital car park. One guard alerted their client to a concern that saved the organisation hundreds of thousands of dollars. Another shared their pride in protecting a well-known global CEO on their visit.

These discussions helped the team to see the 'and' (protecting people *and* assets *and* providing extraordinary service). The customer and employee feedback shifted enormously, all with the support of an incredible leadership team. Feedback from the HR director became some of my most treasured when she shared, 'You have helped to change their hearts and minds'.

As a service leader, you must navigate the team through the journey, listening and validating concerns and never giving up.

How we respond to change

Over many years, I have observed that people fall into categories (illustrated in figure 15) in their response to organisational change.

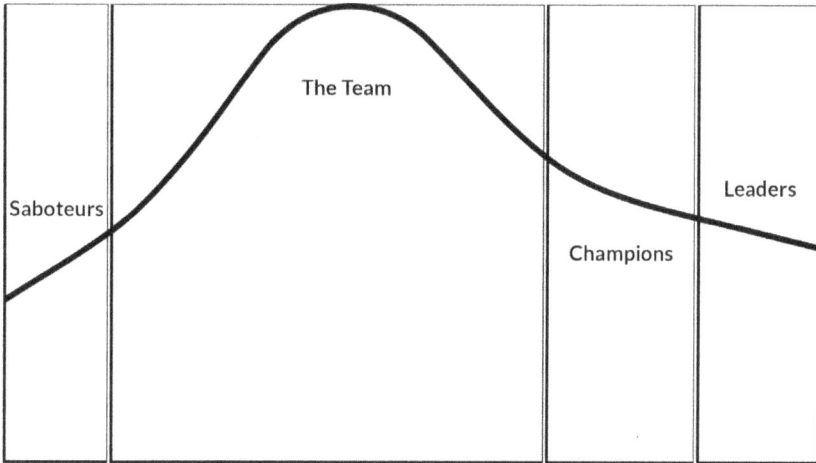

Figure 15: Responses to organisational change

Leaders

The leaders represent those in formal leadership positions, with team members directly reporting to them. These include the CEO, executive, directors, managers, team leaders and anyone responsible for leading others. Leaders are accountable for driving the change they wish to see. Their example, support and championing of change are critical.

Champions

The champions are your supporters and are behind you and the change efforts all the way. They are often referred to as early adopters, keen to be involved, excited and passionate about the service changes and what lies ahead.

The team

The team represents most people in the workforce who show up to work every day to serve their customers. They are committed, open to change and ready to engage and play their roles.

Saboteurs

Saboteurs are not focused on the customer and actively work to undermine any change efforts. They are often negative, destructive, uncooperative and can be very vocal.

As shown in figure 15, saboteurs represent the smallest number of people in an organisation. However, they will try to take the team with them if left unmanaged, so strong leadership is essential.

I always make it my mission not to give up on the saboteurs.

One of my favourite stories is of working with an organisation on a service cultural transformation program. It involved a team member who appeared to be in the saboteur category. He sat at the back of the room and glared at me throughout the entire first session. His face was red and his arms were folded. He looked angry and obviously would have preferred to be anywhere than at the session. He barely participated, and while he wasn't actively disruptive, he was clearly disengaged.

I also worked with the leadership team on service coaching to support team members beyond the initial training. We talked about change and reviewed strategies for getting everyone on board. This was an important link in the change program.

Twelve months later, it was time for the second training session. In walked the disengaged team member. He greeted me and took a seat up the front. He was involved, answered questions and was fully engaged in the session. He even came over during the break and offered me a cup of tea. You can imagine my surprise at the end when he stood and thanked me on behalf of the team for my training workshops and the work done by the leaders over the previous year.

Honestly, you could have knocked me over with a feather.

I carry this lesson with me everywhere. Never give up on people. They can change if they know why, have support and encouragement and are provided with ongoing coaching and reinforcement by caring leaders. They must, of course, be willing.

It is equally important to acknowledge that some people do not want to change, regardless of how many attempts you make. I saw this once in a huge cultural change transformation project. The organisation had made improving customer satisfaction a priority and, with executive leadership support, provided training to the leadership and the frontline.

During one of the first sessions, a disruptive and angry participant raised their hand and said, 'This customer stuff is a load of S$&%!' I hadn't even gotten through the welcome and introduction. During the session, they continued to be disruptive and voice negative opinions despite my best efforts. They did not want to engage and were extremely rude and dismissive.

While this rarely (if ever) needs to happen, I alerted the People and Culture team. If this was how they spoke about customers and felt about customer service, how would it be translated into their service delivery? How would such an attitude to customers rub off on other team members? I was advised that the behaviour the team member had demonstrated in the workshop was a longstanding pattern and nothing had ever been done to address the issue.

This concern also applies to leaders who are not on board with the change. Leaders at any level who are not focused on the customer undermine and inhibit all efforts to shift the service culture. Toxic or unsupportive leadership can destroy a team and culture quicker than any team member will.

As the saying goes, the behaviour we walk past is the behaviour we accept.

I have learnt through extensive experience that performance management is the next step if you have focused on all of the change management strategies, provided support, training and coaching, and that person still doesn't want to be there to look after the customer.

Every leader's goal should be to support team members in the change. But if they do not want to come on board, there must be a different conversation. Otherwise, all other change efforts can be compromised, resulting in a negative experience for the customer and the wider team.

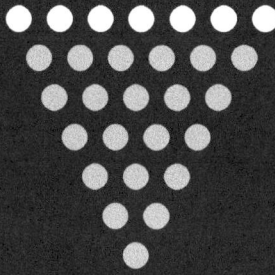

Chapter Summary

Practical tips

- Spend time with the team on the purpose of the change. Understanding the 'why' will make all the difference.

- Acknowledge and validate that change can be difficult.

- Involve the team in change efforts. It makes a massive difference to engagement and the outcome.

- Use the team's ideas and input wherever possible.

- Help the team to see how the change will benefit them.

Reflection questions

- On a scale of 1-10, how would you rate your team's current customer focus level? Do you feel your team does or does not have a customer-focused culture?

- On a scale of 1-10, what is the magnitude of change you envisage in creating a customer-focused culture within your team? What do you want your team to accomplish? What would make you feel proud?

- Which of your team members enjoy change? Which team members find change challenging and may require additional support?

- How can you help your team through the change?

- Have any members of your team been unwilling to change? Does their performance need to be addressed?

Actions to take:

Chapter Eighteen

Managing Performance with Empathy

'The servant as leader always empathizes, always accepts the person, but sometimes refuses to accept some of the person's effort or performance as good enough.'

– Robert Greenleaf

Leaders often ask me, 'How do I address ongoing poor performance?' I acknowledge it can be extremely challenging. That is why leaders need to provide continual recognition and coaching to avoid things getting to this point. It is also where clear goals and service standards help people to know what is expected of them.

It is possible to manage poor performance with empathy. As service leaders, we need to dig deeper to understand why a team member is underperforming in customer service. These reasons may be beyond attitude or effort. That's why we start addressing underperformance with questions such as 'Are you OK? I've noticed you haven't been getting your customer requests completed on time. I'm worried about you.'

This is an important place to start. It's an act of service leadership and more humane than simply telling someone they are not performing. Garry Ridge, the Culture Coach, says, 'In a great organisation, the leaders need to care about their people. Caring has two aspects. One is, I care enough about you to reward you and applaud you doing great work. I'm also brave enough to redirect you when the work you are doing isn't helping you succeed.'

I also believe strongly in zero tolerance for poor or discourteous service.

In their book, *Committing to the Culture: How Leaders Can Create and Sustain Positive Schools*, Steve Gruenert and Todd Whitaker wrote, 'The culture of any organisation is shaped by the worst behavior the leader is willing to tolerate'.[12]

Team members who deliver poor service can negatively affect the organisation with complaints, escalations, financial compensation and legal outcomes, decreased productivity, high turnover, negative social media and word of mouth, reputational damage and the loss of customers, sales or contracts.

I am sure you have heard the expression, 'One bad apple can spoil the bunch'. It's true! Scientists have discovered that ripening fruits emit a gaseous hormone called ethylene that promotes ripening in other fruits. In a literal sense, one ripening apple releases enough ethylene to cause other apples to ripen and eventually rot.

Allowing poor service to continue can have the same impact. Tolerating poor service sends a negative message to the rest of the team. It can significantly impact morale and motivation and cause underperformance and apathy in others. It is frustrating for the team and even more so when leaders don't do anything about it.

The best way to manage underperformance is to ensure it doesn't happen in the first place through thorough selection and recruitment, implementing clear service standards, training and developing the team and providing coaching and ongoing leadership support. This will all help to mitigate poor customer service performance. Prevention is far more important than the cure.

The art of giving feedback

Feedback is an essential tool for every service leader as it can be used for recognition, coaching, and addressing poor performance or service.

If somebody is not delivering the required level of service, the first question a service leader should ask is 'Why?' Every team member must have the chance to succeed through clear goals and standards, training, tools, technology, coaching and support in the first instance. If these are not provided, addressing poor performance is the wrong place to start. If you can confidently say you have enabled the team member, given them every chance to succeed in their role and spent time on service coaching, then it is time to introduce more specific feedback to address poor service.

While coaching and feedback are part of your service leadership tool kit, the art is in knowing which to use and when. Like a golfer selecting the right golf club, the choice makes all the difference to the result. Figure 16 summarises the differences between coaching and feedback.

Coaching	Feedback
Developmental in nature	Can be used during coaching
Can be planned or in the moment	Focused on previous interactions
Question oriented to promote self-discovery	Move directive, telling or advice oriented
Focused on behaviour	Can be positive or constructive
Inquiry oriented, goal is explore options and solutions	Targeted to specific behaviour
Two-way conversations	Can be used to address poor performance

Figure 16: Differences between coaching and feedback

While feedback can be given during coaching and for positive recognition, it is also useful when addressing poor service performance. In this context, it has moved beyond service coaching, where more direct feedback is required.

The SBI™ feedback model

While there are many models of feedback, I have found the SBI™ feedback tool developed by the Center for Creative Leadership (CCL) to be a simple format to deliver effective on-the-spot feedback.[13] It is a widely-recognised model. According to CCL, Situation-Behaviour-Impact™ (SBI™) is proven to reduce the anxiety of delivering feedback and also reduce defensiveness in the recipient.

The SBI™ model allows us to provide feedback in a way that builds trust. It enables us to constructively share our thoughts and feelings, provide clear and specific behavioural examples, and lead responsibility with the individual to take action. It can be used for positive recognition and constructive feedback.

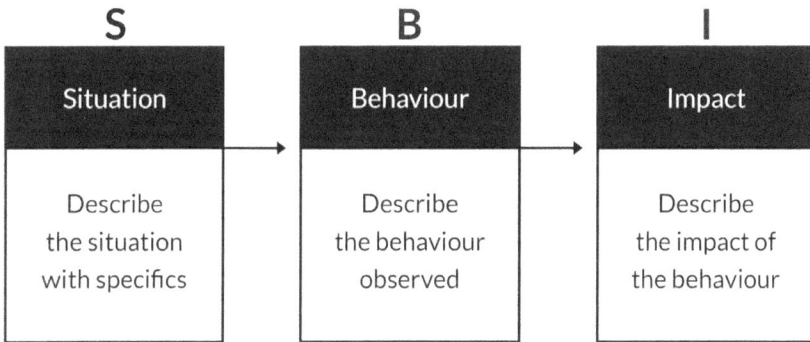

Figure 17: SBI™ model

SBI™ stands for:

Situation

This is where you outline the situation you are referring to so the context is clear and specific.

Behaviour

At this stage, you discuss the exact behaviour you want to address.

Impact

This is an opportunity to highlight the impact of the person's behaviour on the customer, you, the team and the organisation.

It is also clear why referring to the situation, behaviour and impact can be so powerful when giving positive feedback and providing recognition to the team member. Alternatively, when the team member is not performing, it removes the personal aspect and offers a clear structure for delivering feedback.

How to give SBI™ feedback

When using the three stages of the SBI™ feedback tool, it is important to structure your feedback so that it's concise and nonjudgemental. Some service leaders plan this ahead so they are clear and confident about the direction of the conversation. The secret of effective feedback is making it feel like the message is coming from an ally, not an adversary.[14]

As you start the conversation, set things up by sharing your support for the other person, then give them an overview of the situation. This could be a brief check-in.

Situation

When delivering feedback, you must put it in context. Let the person know when and where you observed the situation, so they have a clear reference point. Be as accurate as possible and focus on the facts.

For example, you could say, 'As you know, we have been talking about the importance of punctuality in your role on the phones over the past month and how it affects customer experience. Punctuality is essential and continuing to be late is impacting your performance and ability to be available for our customers.'

Avoid vague or non-specific terms like 'the other day' or 'you are always late'.

Behaviour

The next step is to describe the specific behaviours you want to address. Focus only on those you have observed directly. Describe them accurately with facts.

To continue our example: 'I have noted that over the last two weeks, there have been five occasions when you logged on late for your shift. These time frames have ranged from fifteen minutes to half an hour.'

Avoid making assumptions about someone's behaviour, as you might be wrong, which may undermine your feedback.

Impact

The last stage is to explain the impact of the behaviour you described. If you're providing positive feedback, be clear to demonstrate how the individual's conduct created a positive impact. If you're providing negative feedback, be clear on the negative impact.

Finally, use statements to describe how their behaviour has impacted the customer, you, the team or the organisation. Use 'I' or 'we' to make the point.

For example, you could say: 'Being available for our customers to answer calls, particularly at such a busy time of the year, is so important. When you log on late, it impacts our ability to be there for our customers and puts additional pressure on the rest of the team.'

One more step

We need an additional step after the SBI™ model, which is the opportunity for the team member to respond. This is where we shift from telling mode to listening, as with service coaching. The team member must have time to reflect on your words and respond. This then becomes an open and exploratory conversation and a two-way exchange. Throughout the process, emphasise the importance of finding positive solutions together.

Follow-up is essential after a feedback session to let the team member know you are available for ongoing support where required. Checking in to see how they are progressing shows you care. The outcome of a feedback conversation should be a change or shift in behaviour or customer service performance.

At this stage, document the feedback conversation and also diary a time to follow up.

A word on performance management

Sometimes poor service behaviour continues, and you feel you have exhausted all options through coaching and feedback conversations. If this happens, I recommend referring to your organisation's written performance management policy and seeking assistance from your leader or HR team about going down the path of formal performance management.

While I have found it is rare to need to go this far, at times, it is integral and having the right framework and support in place is vital. It is seldom easy, and professional advice and support will make a difference to the leader and the team member. The bottom line is that poor customer service cannot be tolerated. It is up to every service leader to address underperformance with the right support.

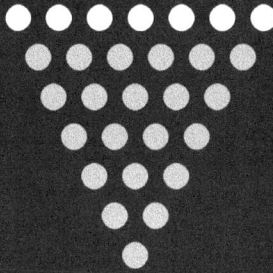

Chapter Summary

Practical tips

- Before the conversation, plan the feedback you will deliver using the SBI™ Model.

- If you find giving feedback challenging, practice with another leader before your conversation with the team member.

- Familiarise yourself with your organisation's performance management policy. Do not allow poor service to continue. Seek further advice if required.

Reflection questions

- What actions do you take on a daily and weekly basis to prevent poor performance in your team?

- Are you fully aware of your organisation's performance management policy?

- Do you currently have any underperforming team members? If so, what help or support do you need from HR/People and Culture?

Actions to take:

PART FIVE
CULTURE

Chapter Nineteen

How to Create an 'All-In' Service Culture

'When every employee in an organisation understands that taking care of the customer is the most important thing they can do, you will have a service culture that will drive your business.'

– John Tschohl

Customer expectations are growing in the commercial, government and not-for-profit sectors. When one organisation raises the bar for customers, everyone is expected to follow. David Mattin, the founder of New World Same Humans, calls it 'expectation transfer'. When businesses take innovative leaps forward, they drive new (higher) expectations among customers.[1]

The impacts of a poor customer experience are significant, and there are multiple costs of poor service. These include complaints and escalations, ombudsman, mediation and legal costs and poor word of mouth (verbal and social media). Customers actively avoid service organisations that deliver negative experiences and are more than willing to share their poor service experiences with others.

Further hidden costs of poor service include labour time associated with re-work, multiple contacts to handle customer issues, and the hours and days of wasted time of people constantly correcting mistakes. Every time a corrective action is required, unnecessary re-work and effort occur.

As we've explored throughout the book, there are also significant costs associated with the employee experience; increased absenteeism, high levels of stress and frustration, poor morale, poor motivation and engagement and, more than ever, attrition and the costs of replacing and retraining employees.

In commercial organisations, service impacts sales and revenue growth, customer retention and loyalty, reputation and profitability. At the highest levels of customer satisfaction, customers become loyal brand advocates, referring and recommending the organisation to family, friends, colleagues and via social media.

Customers no longer base their loyalty on price or product. Instead, they stay loyal to companies based on the experience they receive. Evidence repeatedly shows that loyal customers are easier to serve, typically increase their spend, refer to friends and family and comment via social media, thus increasing their lifetime value.

Poor service leads to lost sales and potential future sales, reduced lifetime value of a customer, churn and loss of customers to competitors and increased advertising and marketing to acquire and re-acquire more customers. Eighty per cent of people say they'd switch to a competitor after more than one bad customer experience.[2]

The emotional and financial impacts of poor customer service are enormous.

Organisations that focus on the customer experience reap multiple benefits at every level across all sectors. These include positive word of mouth, higher customer satisfaction and NPS scores, less re-work and duplication of effort, higher team engagement, team retention and attraction of talent and being an employer of choice.

Consider the following cost savings by focusing on customer experience:

- total savings from reduced rework
- total savings from reduced complaints, escalations, ombudsman and legal costs
- total savings from more accurate information from more knowledgeable people
- total savings from reduced credit notes, discounts and compensation
- total savings from reduced turnover and absenteeism
- total savings from retaining customers
- total savings from increased employee engagement and retention.

The potential return on investment of implementing an organisation-wide focus on the customer experience is significant. A customer-focused culture benefits the customer, the team, the leadership and the organisation.

Where is your customer service culture right now?

What is the service culture like in your organisation? Where do you want it to be? Let's unpack figure 18.

Culture	Focus	Customer Satisfaction
All-In	Sustainability	90%
Committed	Enability	80%
Lip Service	Capability	70%
Disconnected	Leadership	50%
Broken	Standards	-20%

Figure 18: Service culture assessment

Broken

When a service culture is broken, there is a lack of customer focus and customer-centric thinking from the leadership to team members, resulting in a poor customer experience. There are often high levels of customer and employee attrition, lost actual and future business, high customer effort and loss of sales and impact on profitability. Complaints, escalations and brand damage through social media and word of mouth are common.

Disconnected

A disconnected service culture is siloed. The customer is often handballed around the organisation, and no one takes ownership of the customer experience. Internal customer service delivery is poor, and the customer experience is unresponsive and apathetic. A lack of strategic priority around the customer leads to inconsistent experiences.

Lip service

Customer service is often expressed in words but not always backed up by actions. While it is known within the organisation how vital the customer is, it is yet to be ingrained in the service culture. People talk, but there is minimal action.

Committed

There is a commitment to taking care of the customer at leadership, individual and team levels. The leadership, frontline and support teams are dedicated to doing what needs to be done to improve and enhance the customer experience.

All-in

A truly customer-focused organisation gets results. It is embedded in the culture as 'the way we do things around here'. From the customer's perspective, it is a positive, effortless, seamless experience. The customer is at the centre of everyone's thinking. Each leader, individual and department has the customer at the heart of decision-making, processes and daily actions. Customers are loyal, profitability increases and the customer experience is world-class.

The solution is creating buy-in and sustainable customer service from the inside out.

How do you get everyone all-in?

When everyone in the organisation is all-in, there is organisation-wide commitment and responsibility for the customer experience.

Leadership

The level of customer focus a team delivers depends entirely on the leader's customer focus. Every people leader within an organisation is responsible for driving a service culture.

Customer service goes way beyond the customer service department. It is about each business unit focusing strongly on the customer and knowing how their work impacts the end experience. The leadership team ultimately drives the service culture of every organisation.

Frontline

The frontline team is critical to the customer experience. Whether via face-to-face, telephone or digital interactions, they are the face of the company. One thing remains constant: the power of the human experience. No matter how much you invest in technology or research and development, your people will always be your point of difference.

Support office

Everyone in every department (including IT, HR and finance) must focus on the customer and understand their role in the overall customer experience. It's taking care of internal customers, as well as external ones. The quality of the customer's experience will depend on how well people serve each other within the organisation.

Creating an 'all-in' culture can be achieved through a clear service strategy, CEO and executive support, leadership, frontline and support service training, service standards and embedding strategies. Regardless of where a culture is currently, it is possible with commitment and dedication to shift an existing culture to become all-in.

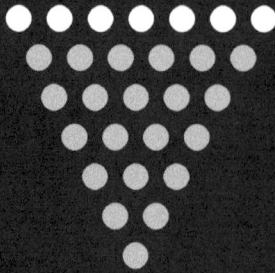

Chapter Summary

Practical tips

- Calculate the costs of poor service for your organisation. How much is poor service costing you annually? Build a business case outlining every identified cost.

- Make customer service a key focus for leadership, the frontline and all support roles in the organisation.

- Start the conversation around examining the existing service culture. Be the change champion if the service culture is not where you believe it should be.

Reflection questions

- Review figure 18. Where is your service culture right now? Where do you want it to be?

- Is everyone in your organisation all-in when it comes to customer focus and care?

- What shift is needed to get everyone focused on the customer experience?

Actions to take:

Chapter Twenty

Creating a Culture of Care

*'Give people not only your
care, but your heart.'*

– Mother Teresa

Caring cultures have people and a human focus at the centre of everything they do. When creating a culture of care, there are three elements: care for self, care for each other, and care for the community.

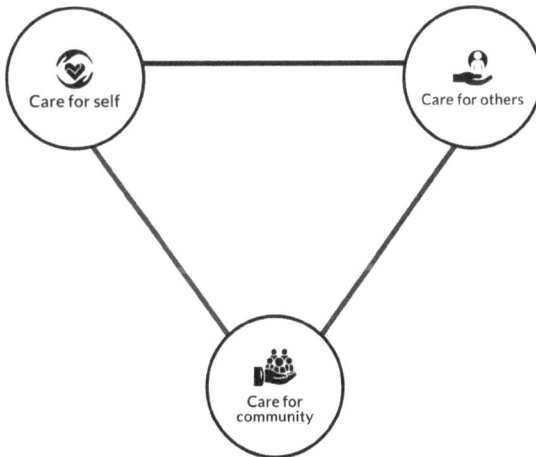

Figure 19: Creating a culture of care

Care for self

'Almost everything will work
again if you unplug it for a few
minutes, including you.'

– Anne Lamott

Service leaders must be committed to caring for themselves to enable them to care for their team and their loved ones outside of work.

I have always highlighted the importance of self-care with customer service professionals to enable them to care for the customer. The same philosophy applies to leadership. In service and service leadership roles, there is a strong focus on serving others. To do so, incorporating self-care into your daily team and leadership practices is essential.

Over the past couple of years, the impact of the pandemic and many changes to the working environment, including physical isolation from teams, increased workload and dealing with increased sick leave and absenteeism, has meant a challenging time for service leaders. This has impacted their self-care.

The words of author Eleanor Brown really resonate with me. 'Rest and self-care are so important. When you take time to replenish your spirit, it allows you to serve from the overflow. You cannot serve from an empty vessel.'

I always ask service leaders, 'Are you creating time and space to take care of yourself?' The answer is often a resounding 'No'. I make no judgement here, as taking time to care for ourselves is not always easy. Yet the benefits are enormous for everyone. Is there anything more powerful for a team to see than leaders taking care of themselves? It gives the team permission to do the same. A leader who demonstrates self-care has far more impact than simply telling their team to focus on self-care strategies.

Recently a team member shared, 'We have a leader who tells us to focus on our self-care, then they work every night late at the office and spend all weekend sending us emails'. Their message is incongruent with their actions and impacts the teams' ability to focus on their own self care.

In *Stress and Its Relationship to Leadership and a Healthy Workplace Culture*, researchers Ross, Exposito and Kennedy write about the effects of stress on leaders. 'If a leader experiences stress, neurotransmitters and hormones are released and the leader may experience a short period of increased focus and reaction time. But if the stress exists for a long enough period of time, there will be negative consequences. Characteristics of these negative behaviours include (a) lack of listening, (b) over-analysis, (c) failure to make decisions, and (d) erratic, fearful or angry emotional decisions.'[3]

Leadership self-care includes caring for the mind, body and soul. Your mind is your most powerful tool, and ensuring it has time to rest is vital. Your body is the vehicle that enables you to do what you have to do. Yet most of us take better care of servicing and maintaining our cars than our bodies. Physical health needs our attention. And then there is the soul. I think of the soul as our essence, our true nature.

Remember that every principle of leadership self-care applies equally to your team.

Self-care can look different for different people. Regardless of the activity, it is a leadership philosophy, a mindset, and a practical application. And most importantly, it is about working out what works for you.

The quadrant of self-care

In my service and leadership training, I focus on the quadrant of self-care practices: physical, daily routine, connection and mindset. They are practical ideas for use on an ongoing basis, designed to help leaders to focus on themselves. As service leaders give so much to others, giving time to replenish, restore and refocus themselves is essential.

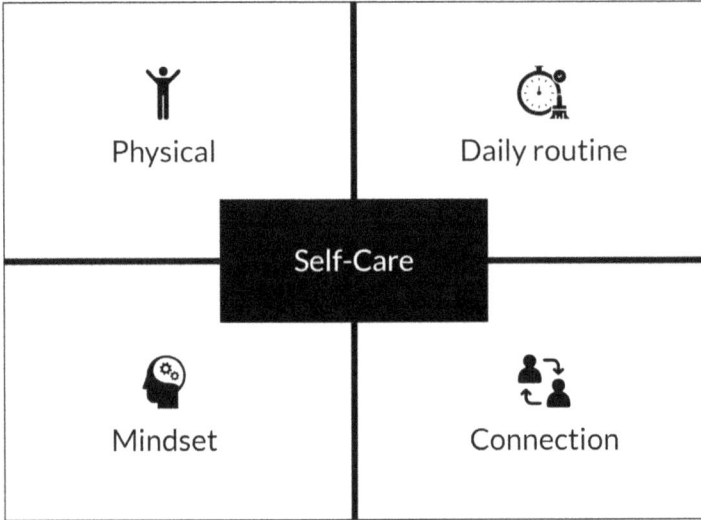

Figure 20: The quadrant of self-care

Physical

The physical component of the self-care quadrant involves what we can do physically to care for ourselves. These include:

Box breathing

Box breathing is a form of deep breathing utilised by stressed people everywhere. It's also known as sama vritti pranayama, born of the yogic practice of pranayama, or focusing on the breath.

Box breathing is a timed technique with a set rhythm that can reduce stress. It is often referred to as four-square breathing and is simple to practice. Get comfortable, then do the following.

- Let all the breath in your lungs out to the count of four.
- Hold your breath for four counts.
- Take four quick deep breaths.
- Hold that breath for four counts.
- Repeat.

Use this any time throughout the day if you are feeling stressed or overwhelmed; it truly does work!

Sleep routine

While we all need varying amounts of sleep, having adequate rest and sleep is important. While it isn't always possible (as the mother of four children, I know sleep deprivation all too well!), consciously planning a good night's sleep can be crucial to wellbeing. Even though you might not be aware of it, the amount and quality of sleep you get each night impacts several factors, including your immune system and how your mood is affected.

Consistently getting enough sleep can benefit your health in all respects. Wherever possible, establish a sleep schedule. This entails a regular wake-up time, winding down or preparing for bed, and a regular time to sleep. Your circadian rhythm, the physiological procedure your body uses to control your sleep and waking cycle, depends on it. Try putting your phone, tablet, alarm clock, and other electrical devices on the opposite side of the room or, better still, outside your room. Doing this can prevent distractions or being woken up in the middle of the night.

Set an alarm to remind you of your scheduled bedtime. And finally, have a period of time away from screens before bedtime to improve the chances of a good night's sleep.

Exercise routine

The key to exercise is planning it into your day or week and choosing to do something you love. For some, that may be going to the gym, while for others, it could be walking, yoga, pilates or catching up with friends for a walk and talk. Using your lunch break to exercise can be good if you have a busy schedule and competing priorities. Exercise is the foundation of good mental and physical health. It is about the discipline of making it happen in your weekly schedule.

Water

Remember throughout the day to hydrate your cells. We cannot survive without water. It is essential for numerous bodily processes, such as supplying nutrition to cells, eliminating waste, safeguarding joints and organs, and regulating body temperature. It is also crucial for your voice. Have a bottle of water beside you. There is even an app to remind you to drink water regularly throughout the day.

Energy audit

One of the most useful concepts I have ever heard regarding energy management is from a wonderful mentor, Col Fink. He taught me the idea of doing an energy audit. Basically, you take a piece of paper and draw two columns. At the top of one, you write 'gives me energy', and the other is 'zaps my energy'. Rather than focusing on time management, it is about energy management. You list everything in life (both work and outside of work) that gives you energy and then commit to doing more of that. List what zaps your energy (both work and outside work), then do whatever is possible to eliminate or reduce those things. This activity is worth doing regularly or if you are feeling low on energy!

Daily routine

Daily routines consist of what we schedule. The trick is putting them in your diary, just as you would important meetings or deadlines. These include:

Taking breaks

I am a huge advocate of structured breaks away from the desk or office. This stems from my days on the phones, when morning tea, lunch and afternoon tea breaks were scheduled at the start of the day. I use this in training and strongly encourage service leaders and team members to take regular breaks. We all need time to rest and rejuvenate, as it affects levels of concentration and focus.

This is particularly important when working from home. Planned breaks throughout the day will ensure you have time to switch off and refocus.

60-minute stretch breaks

With more time spent at our desks, on Zoom or in virtual meetings, some days feel like we are stuck to our chairs! Use a standing desk or a fit ball, or stand up and stretch every sixty minutes to avoid getting stiff. Mobile headsets are useful for walking and talking, as are walking meetings. Use the reminder on your phone, watch or app to stand up and move.

Practising daily gratitude

I have practised gratitude every day since learning of the benefits through the work of Martin Seligman. He is known as the father of positive psychology, and his book *Learned Optimism* is well worth reading.[4] Every night at our family dinner table, we share the best part of our day and what we are most grateful for. With a family of seven (my darling mum lives with us), this can descend into connected conversations, chaos and often much laughter, but it has been enormously helpful and a practice that has continued in our home for more than twenty years. There are numerous immediate and long-term advantages to regularly practising and expressing gratitude. Evidence supports that those who intentionally focus on daily gratitude have improved mental health.[5]

According to studies, those with a propensity for gratitude exhibit higher levels of brain activity in the medial prefrontal cortex, which is connected to learning and judgement. In one study, this brain activity was present a month after the test, indicating that the impacts of appreciation lingered.

Gratitude is the practice of acknowledging others for their kindness or the positive aspects of our existence. Start and end the day with gratitude. Mentally note, or even write down, three things you are grateful for.

Daily digital consumption awareness

Devices can be a source of connection with family and friends but can also lead to endless scrolling and wasted time. I am also guilty of this (especially Instagram reels of cute puppies!). Having healthy boundaries with social media and being aware of what we consume is important for mental health. Focusing on comparisons or reading news stories of constant negativity can play havoc.

Make time for hobbies and interests

What do you love doing outside of work? What brings you joy and lights you up? I'm always fascinated by the variety of what people love to do in their spare time. With the demands of leading teams and life in general, finding time for hobbies and interests can be difficult.

I recommend scheduling it at the start of the week or month to ensure it is a priority. Whether it's reading, cooking, the outdoors or yoga, fill your cup every week. One of my favourite examples was a brilliant customer experience manager whose hobby was cake decorating. While he was busy getting incredible results at work, transforming technology platforms and improving customer and team satisfaction, he still made time for baking and proudly shared his magnificent creations.

Connection

Humans are wired for connection. We all have different preferences; some are extroverted and energised by being with people, while others are introverted and prefer to recharge with time alone. But making time for connection is essential in our busy lives.

Encourage connection – who could you reach out to?

Service leaders need to know when team members need additional help and support. They could be going through a challenging time outside work, grieving or navigating difficult personal circumstances. People are not always good at asking for help, so saying, 'Please let me know if you need anything' is not enough. Rather than waiting for them to approach you, proactively reach out and see how you can help or support them. This extends beyond the team and may involve anyone within the organisation.

Be proactive in speaking up if you need help – who could help you?

Some things are difficult to navigate alone. Being a leader is not easy, and it may be *you* who needs additional help or support from a trusted friend or advisor, an external resource, the organisation's employee assistance program or a fellow leader. Remember, you are never alone, and there will always be someone who can support you.

Create connection

In the busyness of life, weeks and months fly by before we know it. Making time for connection with our family and friends and spending time with pets and others who bring us joy is enormously valuable. Whether that is scheduling a monthly date night with your partner or best friend, organising the annual family get-together or holiday, or simply walking the dog each day. It is far more likely to happen if it is in your diary. We all need connection and time with those who rejuvenate us. Schedule it and make it happen.

Make time for weekly team connection

I encourage all service leaders to make time each week to connect without an agenda. It could be sharing morning tea, having fun or a competition. One team I worked with loved doing the crossword together, while another brought food from their cultural backgrounds for a shared lunch. Scheduling team activities outside of work can also be a lot of fun. I work with teams that have team dinners, play lawn bowls, sing karaoke, go on picnics and play mini-golf. The options are endless. Being together in a relaxed environment that is not focused on work can create a deeper connection and a sense of belonging.

Mindset

Your mindset is crucial in dealing with life's challenges inside and outside work. It needs to be protected, just as you would wear a helmet when riding a bicycle.

The 90-second rule

As a lifelong learner, I attended a four-day *Unleash the Power Within* event with personal development author Tony Robbins.[6] One of the most useful tools I learnt was the 90-second rule.

Robbins describes this as how long you give yourself to recover after an incident or something that upsets or annoys you. Basically, after the incident occurs, you allow yourself 90 seconds to be angry or upset and then choose to let it go. From then on, you choose not to dwell on the situation or person or spend more time or energy thinking about it.

On first hearing, I thought this sounded fine in theory, but putting it into practice would be more challenging. The next morning at breakfast, someone pushed in front of me at the hotel omelette bar. Two things annoyed me; first, it was poor manners, and second, this person was getting in the way of my eating! I remember the anger welling up and thinking, 'How rude is that!' I decided to put the 90-second rule into practice. And it worked.

I have found this rule useful for life in general. It can apply to partners, family, pets or even when someone cuts you off in traffic. And it is something I have to continue to work on!

I also know that sometimes we need additional help if we hang onto things and find it difficult to let go. Sometimes we may be dealing with more complex or difficult issues. If that is the case, seek professional help or support.

Choose your response

One of the most empowering beliefs you can adopt is choosing your response in any given situation. In the words of the late Dr Stephen Covey: 'Ultimately, this power to choose is what defines us as human beings. We may have limited choices, but we can always choose. We can choose our thoughts, emotions, moods, our words, our actions; we can choose our values and live by principles. It is the choice of acting or being acted upon'.

In his bestselling book, *The 7 Habits of Highly Effective People*, Covey talks about the space between stimulus (what happens) and response (reaction). There, we always have the power to choose. It's like a giant pause button. We don't have to react to every stimulus; instead, we can pause, reflect, and choose our response. This is a useful reminder for any service leader when dealing with challenging situations and applies equally outside work.[7]

Create a daily meditation practice

Meditation is a mind-body practice in which your attention is focused on being mindful of the present, your breath and your mind to promote awareness, cultivate wellbeing and reduce stress and anxiety.[8]

Daily meditation, the practice of staying present and mindful for a limited period, has numerous mental and physical health benefits. These include reducing stress, lowering blood pressure, strengthening the immune system, improving memory, concentration and focus, and improving sleep and overall mood.

A useful place to start is with a morning or evening meditation practice (or both). Try using apps like Headspace or Smiling Mind to get started.

Care for each other

Care for each other extends to care for the team, customers (both external and internal), suppliers and partners. 'Caring is no longer a luxury, rather a necessity to elevate our individual and collective wellbeing.'[9] Caring is an integral component of basic human life, demonstrated through what we say and do as service leaders.

Care is a 'doing' word, demonstrated through words and actions. It can be how we respond to another when they ask for our help. It could be ensuring our work is accurate and correct the first time. Or the care we put into an email response. Care is valuing and appreciating differences. Showing care can be finding out what our customers need and then delivering it. It is the thoughtful follow-up after a problem or issue.

Care is fostering a culture through leadership and service to others.

Care for community

Organisations measure success through their balance sheet and the bottom line and also through social and environmental performance, accountability and transparency. People are more socially and environmentally conscious. In a study by PWC, 75% of employees said they wanted to work for an organisation that positively contributes to society.[10]

Socially responsible businesses attract customers and talent and have higher engagement opportunities for customers and employees.

In addition, it turns out that consumers are also happy to pay more for products from companies that give back to society.[11]

Companies that care about their communities and support those in need do so in different ways. Some give back through monetary donations, while others create sustainable products that reduce harm to the planet. This includes companies that care about sustainability, diversity and inclusion.

Timothy Calkins, clinical professor of marketing at the Kellogg School of Management, wrote, 'Consumers really want to know that a company cares. Given all the uncertainty in the world right now and all the risk and the hazard and the way people are feeling, there's nothing more important'.[12]

A global example of a company taking care of its community is the Hilton Hotel. The company granted more than US$1 million in October 2020 through its Hilton Effect Foundation to support grassroots community groups helping the disadvantaged and homeless who were severely impacted by the pandemic.[13]

'We're all interconnected and can help one another during challenging times,' says Terence Lester, executive director of Love Beyond Walls, which received a grant from the hotel.

Hilton also helped thousands of medical professionals on the front lines with its One Million Rooms initiative, providing free stays at hotels across the country.

'Hilton became my family while I was here,' says Natalie Morreale, an ER nurse who worked in New York City for two months. 'Hotel staffers would greet us with a smile, with a nice sign or note, and just say thank you. This is not an experience I will ever forget, and the Hilton team really made it possible in so many ways.'[14]

Hilton consistently rates in the list of best places to work globally.

We all need more care

Robert Greenleaf recognised that organisations, as well as individuals, could be servant-leaders. He believed that servant-leader organisations could change the world. In his second major essay, *The Institution as Servant*, written in 1976, Greenleaf articulated what is often called the 'credo'.[15]

'This is my thesis: caring for persons, the more able and the less able serving each other, is the rock upon which a good society is built. Whereas, until recently, caring was largely person-to-person, now most of it is mediated through institutions – often large, complex, powerful, impersonal; not always competent; sometimes corrupt. If a better society is to be built, one that is more just and more loving, one that provides more creative opportunity for its people, then the most open course is to raise both the capacity to serve and the very performance as servant of existing major institutions by new regenerative forces operating within them.'

Our world desperately needs more care. It starts with how we care for ourselves as leaders and how we care for others, be they our team, colleagues or customers, and extends to the care of our community. Organisations and leaders who care significantly impact those around them, make a difference in our world, and the ripple effect is enormous.

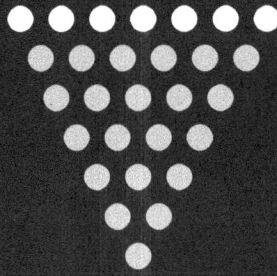

Chapter Summary

Practical tips

- Diarise self-care as you would any important meeting or appointment.

- Review the quadrant of self-care and choose to focus on any area that would help you as a service leader.

- Create opportunities for team members to volunteer for your organisation's defined charity or one that matters to the team member.

Reflection questions

- At the start of each day or week, ask, 'What will I commit to as an act of self-care?'

- At the end of every day, ask yourself, 'What have I done to care for myself today?'

- How well are you encouraging self-care practices in your team?

Actions to take:

Leadership Action Plan

'Action is the foundational
key to all success.'

– Pablo Picasso

Using the actions you have created at the end of each chapter, it is time to formulate your action plan for the next twelve months. The Stop, Start, Change and Continue model is a useful technique here. Consider what you have learnt throughout the book.

Stop: What are you doing that you would like to stop because it is not adding value or contributing to your service leadership?

Start: What ideas have you generated that you are not currently using but would impact your team or service leadership capability?

Change: What changes do you need to make in the short and long term?

Continue: What is working well for you as a service leader that you will continue to focus on?

Date:

Stop	Start
Change	**Continue**

Make sure to review your action plan and track it regularly. Look for quick wins and prioritise those actions that will have the biggest impact.

Your Leadership Legacy

'The true mark of a leader is measured
by the lives that leader touches.'

– Sinive Seely

One of my first corporate jobs was working as a customer service representative for Optus. The company had recently come into the market as the first competitor to Telstra, and there was an incredible focus on taking care of people and taking care of the customers. Then-CEO Bob Mansfield OAM led the initiative.

Bob was much-loved and known to be incredibly approachable.

He used to walk the floors. We had two head offices, one in Melbourne and one in Sydney. When Bob visited from Sydney, he made time to meet and get to know everyone from the frontline, team leaders and managers.

On one particular shift, I was waiting for a call when I looked up and saw Bob Mansfield approaching my desk. I was star-struck, knowing who he was and the position he held. He introduced himself and we chatted when the phone suddenly rang. I froze, feeling conflicted about what to do next. Should I pick up the call? Should I keep talking? Would it be rude if I picked up the call? As my internal dialogue raced, Bob sensed my hesitation and said, 'It's all good, just pick up the phone.'

He remained by my desk while I spoke with the customer. Fortunately, it wasn't a complex call, but still mildly nerve-racking with the CEO listening! I completed the call and Bob said, with genuine interest, 'So tell me, how was the customer? Were they happy?' I shared my experience of the customer conversation. Bob thanked me for my time and continued on his way.

In that moment, he showed that the customer was most important, not him.

When Bob Mansfield announced his departure, people cried in the corridors. Such was the power of his leadership and how he made people feel. He always showed the importance of the customer and the team in actions, not just words. I carry that lesson with me always.

Although it has been nearly thirty years since Bob Mansfield held that position, people in my Service Leadership programs still mention his name when I ask about the most customer-focused leader they have ever known.

My dear friend and colleague, Annmarie Carroll, is an HR consultant. She has been one of my greatest inspirations in customer service, encouraging me to pursue my career in training and development. She shared her memories of working with Bob.

> 'As a young corporate HR professional, being a part of and watching a telco grow from the ground up in Melbourne gave me incredible insight into the power of inspiring leadership. CEO Bob Mansfield provided complete transparency and authenticity to the young and enthusiastic workforce that generated immediate trust and commitment in this fast-growing start-up workforce. His honest communication sessions every week were televised live, bravely providing the opportunity for any staff member to call and ask a 'live' question. I was fascinated to see that no matter how busy the floors of the corporate centre building were, everyone would stop their meeting or move to a tv screen to listen to Bob's weekly update.
>
> He made every individual feel valued and essential to the business. Central to our organisational purpose was a customer focus that built a company culture that was impossible to match by our main competitor.

This customer focus permeated our leadership decisions, hiring, training, values and language. Every win was celebrated, and every failure was seen as a learning experience. His energy lifted the training floor I managed every time he walked through the door — always unannounced, always motivated with his sleeves rolled up! He had a gift for remembering everyone's name and would never forget to thank the teams or individuals he came into contact with.

Bob's departure from the organisation proved that some people are not replaceable. I watched the next CEOs come and go and the energy and customer focus of the organisation start to wane as short-term profitability became the driver. My own leadership style was influenced by Bob's values, the importance of kindness, transparency and acknowledgment and power of the individual, be they a customer, co-worker, executive, board member, cleaner or delivery person.'

Imagine that being written about you as a leader thirty years later.

I am reminded of the words of Raj Sisodia, co-author of *Conscious Capitalism*, 'The success of a leader is best gauged by what happens after they are gone'.[1]

In the busyness of taking care of teams, people, tasks, and demands, it is sometimes easy to forget the impact of service leaders. Yet I continue to see and hear of that impact and the difference they make in the lives of others.

So, fast forward to five, ten, twenty or even thirty years from now.

What will your leadership legacy be?

How do you want to be remembered?

What difference did you make to the people you met and the lives you touched?

We all leave a legacy — whenever we go. I learnt this from the leaders I have known and my own family. That includes my dear Dad and my sisters Natasha and Simone, who departed this world far too early but left an indelible mark on many lives.

Maybe you will work for one company, maybe for many.

Maybe you have your own business or will build your own in the future.

Regardless of the company or the industry you work in, as a service leader, how you lead will impact you and future generations. As Max De Pree wrote in *Leadership is an Art*, 'Leaders should leave behind them assets and a legacy'.[2]

Take some time to go to a quiet place and reflect. Think about the legacy you will leave for your team, your organisation and your customers. Write it in the space below and keep it close to you.

May it guide you in everything you do.

My Leadership Vision

Write down your leadership vision. How do you want to be remembered?

Afterword

My hope is that after reading this book, you have created a series of actions from each chapter to apply and improve your skills as a service leader. At the same time, I hope you have been able to reflect on your many strengths and acknowledge all the wonderful things you are already doing with your team. In a society obsessed with constant improvement and development, sometimes we fail to sit back and appreciate everything we have already done and give ourselves a pat on the back and some well-deserved recognition. Reflect on all you are already doing.

Service leadership is a lifelong and continuing commitment full of opportunities to learn, explore and make mistakes. Learning from those mistakes is a chance to be inspiring and inspired each day. It is a pledge to turn up to work with a servant's heart, be committed to our teams and be the best version of ourselves. It is learning, falling down, getting back up again and recognising the responsibility we have every day to take care of our people, each other and our community.

It is promising to take care of ourselves because if we don't, nothing else will work.

My life's work has been developing people working in the customer service industry, including the frontline, support team and leaders. It is my greatest passion, and even after all these years, I still wake up every day excited, ready to bounce out of bed and work with incredible clients.

My continued work is in service leadership, developing current and future leaders and working with organisations on building sustainable service cultures through a long-term commitment to learning and development.

My next book is already in the early stages of planning. It links leadership with creating a sustainable 'all-in' service culture. That involves every person in the organisation and is a long-term commitment to creating a world-class organisation and customer experience. When we are 'all-in', we have the most significant impact on the team, the customers, the leadership, the culture, and the desired outcomes. And it is all about creating results.

Sometimes leaders may feel alone in their journeys. I invite you to connect with me on LinkedIn and reach out to me at hello@moniquerichardson. com.au with any questions or if I may be of service to you, your team or your organisation. You are also welcome to join our service leadership community. Please scan the QR code to join my weekly service insights newsletter.

I have wanted to write this book for many years, as I promised the frontline I would ensure their voices were heard. This book supports the many incredible service leaders in our customer service community across the globe, making a difference to team members and customers every day.

I look forward to staying connected and continuing our learning journey together.

About the Author

Monique Richardson is a leading international expert in service leadership and customer service whose goal is to help transform customer service cultures through a service leadership-driven approach. Creating a truly customer-focused culture is about putting people first and focusing on the employee experience to ensure a highly engaged and empowered workforce and provide the best customer experiences possible.

Over two decades as a keynote speaker and trainer, Monique has delivered workshops to over 50,000 people. Monique is the author of *Managing Difficult Customer Behaviour – A Practical Guide for Confident Conversations*. She offers workshops and regularly speaks at conferences across the globe. Her thoughts have featured on Sky News, Sunrise, CEO World, The CEO Institute, Business Essentials Daily and Team Guru.

Monique's amazing clients are varied; she has designed and delivered programs for many ASX top 200 companies and works extensively with clients in the commercial, government and not-for-profit sectors. She partners with organisations to design and deliver bespoke training programs in the areas of service transformation, service leadership, service excellence and service recovery.

As a conference speaker, Monique brings experience, passion, excitement and humour to the stage. If you are organising a conference and are looking for a speaker who will engage and inspire your audience to take action, please contact Monique at hello@moniquerichardson.com.au

Monique is a proud wife and mother of four children (and one fur baby) and lives in Melbourne, Victoria. She is passionate about creating a more caring world, family, food, fundraising through her 'Love, Hope and Daisies' foundation and always having fun.

hello@moniquerichardson.com.au
www.moniquerichardson.com.au
+61 402 113 912

Love, Hope and Daisies Foundation

The Love, Hope and Daisies Foundation was established in loving memory of my beautiful younger sister Simone, who passed away in 1999, aged 21. Simone's life, although far too brief, had a significant impact. She made a huge difference in so many people's lives through her love and care for everyone she came into contact with.

The Foundation is all about making a difference wherever there is a need, either through financial donations, fundraising efforts or gifts of time. I am a proud supporter of St Mary's House of Welcome, which provides services to people who are homeless and experiencing poverty, severe and persistent mental health issues and those who are socially marginalised. Five per cent of all profits from my business are donated directly to St Mary's House of Welcome, and we involve friends, family and the community in various fundraising efforts.

The foundation symbol is how Simone used to sign off each letter she wrote to her friends and family.

Ten per cent of all profits from the sale of this book will be donated directly to St Mary's House of Welcome. Learn more about them at www.smhow.org.au

Love, hope and daisies
FOUNDATION

References

Foreword

1.   Wigert, B. (2022). The Top 6 Things Employees Want in Their Next Job. *Gallup.com*. https://www.gallup.com/workplace/389807/top-things-employees-next-job.aspx

Chapter One

1.   Greenleaf, R. (2015). *The Servant as Leader*. Revised edn. The Greenleaf Center for Servant Leadership.

2.   Cable, D. (2018, April 23). How Humble Leadership Really Works. *Harvard Business Review*. https://hbr.org/2018/04/how-humble-leadership-really-works

3.   Blanchard, K.H. and Broadwell, R. (2018). *Servant Leadership in Action: How you can achieve great relationships and results*. Berrett-Koehler Publishers.

4.   The Greenleaf Center for Servant Leadership. *What is Servant Leadership?* https://www.greenleaf.org/what-is-servant-leadership/

5.   Spears, L.C. (2004). Practicing servant-leadership. *Leader to Leader*, 2004 (34), pp.7–11.

Chapter Two

6.   De Pree, M. (2004). *Leadership Is An Art*. Currency.

7.   Schulze, H. & Merrill, D. (2019). *Excellence Wins: A no-nonsense guide to becoming the best in a world of compromise*. Zondervan.

8.   Suner, E. (2020, February 6). Why Leaders Should Focus on Strengths Not Weaknesses. *Forbes*. www.forbes.com/sites/

forbescoachescouncil/2020/02/06/why-leaders-should-focus-on-strengths-not-weaknesses/?sh=4e387acf3d1a

9.   Blanchard, K. & Broadwell, R. (2018). *Servant Leadership in Action: How you can achieve great relationships and results.* Polvera Publishing.

10. Brower, R. (2021, September 19). Empathy Is The Most Important Leadership Skill. Forbes. https://www.forbes.com/sites/tracybrower/2021/09/19/empathy-is-the-most-important-leadership-skill-according-to-research/?sh=1dc91c2f3dc5

11. Hougaard, R., Carter, J, & Afton, M. (2021, December 23). Connect With Empathy But Lead With Compassion. *Harvard Business Review.* https://hbr.org/2021/12/connect-with-empathy-but-lead-with-compassion

12. Blanchard, K. Ken Blanchard - Servant Leadership [Video]. *London Business Forum.* https://video.londonbusinessforum.com/detail/videos/inspire-me/video/5441184700001/ken-blanchard---servant-leadership?autoStart=true

Chapter Three

13. Carlzon, J. (1989). *Moments of Truth.* Harper Business.

14. Heskett, J.L., Jones, T.O., Loveman, G.W., Sasser, W.E. & Schlesinger, L.A. (2008, July-August). Putting the Service-Profit Chain to Work. *Harvard Business Review.* https://hbr.org/2008/07/putting-the-service-profit-chain-to-work

Chapter Four

1.   Pendell, R. (2022, June 14). The World's $7.8 Trillion Workplace Problem. *Gallup.* https://www.gallup.com/workplace/393497/world-trillion-workplace-problem.aspx

2.   Cloud, H. (2016). *The Power Of The Other: The startling effect other people have on you, from the boardroom to the bedroom and beyond-and what to do about it.* Harper Business.

3.   Yohn, D. (2019, June 13). Why Every Company Needs A Chief Experience

Officer, *Harvard Business Review*. https://hbr.org/2019/06/why-every-company-needs-a-chief-experience-officer

4. Accenture. (2018, June 13). https://bankingblog.accenture.com/making-the-connection-between-cx-and-ex-a-recipe-for-competitive-advantage

5. Ravinutala, R. (2022, April 29). Breaking Down Silos To Create A 360-Degree Total Experience Strategy Through Conversational AI, *Forbes*. https://www.forbes.com/sites/forbestechcouncil/2022/04/29/breaking-down-silos-to-create-a-360-degree-total-experience-strategy-through-conversational-ai/?sh=780680aa3a22

6. Ibid.

7. Heskett, J.L, Jones, T.O., Loveman, G.W., Sasser W.E., & Schlesinger L.A. (2008, July-August). Putting the Service-Profit Chain to Work. *Harvard Business Review*. https://hbr.org/2008/07/putting-the-service-profit-chain-to-work

8. Ravinutala, R. (2022, April 29). Breaking Down Silos To Create A 360-Degree Total Experience Strategy Through Conversational AI. *Forbes*. https://www.forbes.com/sites/forbestechcouncil/2022/04/29/breaking-down-silos-to-create-a-360-degree-total-experience-strategy-through-conversational-ai/?sh=780680aa3a22

Chapter Six

9. Haycock, L. (2022, March 23). The Cost To Hire An Employee Might Be Higher Than You Think. *HRM*. https://www.hrmonline.com.au/section/featured/cost-of-hiring-new-employee/

10. Shear, L. (2021, September 21). The Empathy Economy: Care, so your customers will too. *Zendesk*. https://www.zendesk.com/au/blog/empathy-economy-care-customers-will too/#georedirect

11. Perry, B.D. & Szalavitz, M. (2011). *Born for Love: Why Empathy is Essential - and Endangered*. William Morrow Paperbacks.

12. Clinton, D. (2018, February 8). Automation will make customer service the most in-demand job in tech. *Business Insider*. https://www.

businessinsider.com/automation-will-make-customer-service-the-most-in-demand-job-in-tech-2018-2

13. Cockburn, G. (2020, August 6). Retail workers suffer as grumpy customers lash out over COVID-19 restrictions. *news.com.au*. https://www.news.com.au/finance/business/retail/retail-workers-suffer-as-grumpy-customers-lash-out-over-covid19-restrictions/news-story/2b87e382b38ab6f76f33d39dad354d1-2

Chapter Seven

14. Oracle. (n.d.). What is Onboarding? https://www.oracle.com/au/human-capital-management/talent-management/what-is-onboarding/

15. Wetherell, E. & Nelson, B. (2021, August 12). 8 Practical Tips for Leaders for a Better Onboarding Process. *Gallup*. https://www.gallup.com/workplace/353096/practical-tips-leaders-better-onboarding-process.aspx

16. Carucci, R. (2018, October 29). When Companies Should Invest In Training Their Employees and When They Shouldn't. *Harvard Business Review*. https://hbr.org/2018/10/when-companies-should-invest-in-training-their-employees-and-when-they-shouldnt

Chapter Eight

17. Qualtrics XM. (n.d.). Your ultimate guide to employee engagement. *Qualtrics XM*. https://www.qualtrics.com/au/experience-management/employee/engagement-engagement-guide/?rid=ip&prevsite=en&newsite=au&geo=AU&geomatch=au

18. Younger, H.R. (2017). *The 7 Intuitive Laws of Employee Loyalty*. LeadU Publishing.

19. Martin, R. L. (2022, March-April). The Real Secret to Retaining Talent. *Harvard Business Review*. https://hbr.org/2022/03/the-real-secret-to-retaining-talent

20. PricewaterhouseCoopers. (2022, May, 24). Global Workforce Hopes and

Fears Survey. *PwC*. https://www.pwc.com/gx/en/issues/workforce/hopes-and-fears-2022.html

21. Martin, M. (2021, June 21). Valuable Employee Engagement Statistics In 2021. *The Circular Board*. https://thecircularboard.com/employee-engagement-statistics/

22. Moss, J. (2021). Beyond Burned Out. *Harvard Business Review*. https://hbr.org/2021/02/beyond-burned-out

23. Henley, D. (2022, March 20). The Secret to Creating a Sense of Belonging at Work. *Forbes*. https://www.forbes.com/sites/dedehenley/2022/03/20/the-secret-to-creating-a-sense-of-belonging-at-work/

24. Carr, E.W., Reece, A., Kellerman, G.R. & Robichaux, A. (2019, December 16). The Value of Belonging at Work. *Harvard Business Review*. https://hbr.org/2019/12/the-value-of-belonging-at-work

25. Henley, D. (2022, March 20). The Secret to Creating a Sense of Belonging at Work. *Forbes*. https://www.forbes.com/sites/dedehenley/2022/03/20/the-secret-to-creating-a-sense-of-belonging-at-work/?sh=706eb59c7a88

Chapter Nine

26. HR Onboard. (2015). Offboarding is more important than you think. https://hronboard.me/blog/offboarding-is-more-important-than-you-think-infographic/

27. Wigert, B. & Agrawal, S. (2019, February 19). 3 Ways to Create a Positive Exit Experience for Your Employees. *Gallup*. https://www.gallup.com/workplace/246203/ways-create-positive-exit-experience-employees.aspx

Chapter Eleven

28. Newland, S. (2018). The Power of Accountability. *ACFPE*. https://www.afcpe.org/news-and-publications/the-standard/2018-3/the-power-of-accountability/

Chapter Twelve

1. Lee, A., Willis, S. & Tian, A. (2018). When Empowering Employees Works and When It Doesn't. *Harvard Business Review.* https://hbr.org/2018/03/when-empowering-employees-works-and-when-it-doesnt

2. Brown, B. (2018). *Dare to Lead: Brave Work. Tough Conversations. Whole Hearts.* Random House.

3. Spector, R. & Reeves, B.O. (2017). *The Nordstrom Way to Customer Experience Excellence: Creating a values-driven service culture.* John Wiley & Sons.

Chapter Thirteen

4. Cable, D. (2018). How Humble Leadership Really Works. *Harvard Business Review* https://hbr.org/2018/04/how-humble-leadership-really-works

5. Qualtrics XM. (n.d.). People Leader's Guide: 2021 Employee Experience Trends. *Qualtrics XM.* https://www.qualtrics.com/ebooks-guides/employee-experience-trends-2021/

6. Ibid.

7. Bersin, J. (2021, May 15). Voice Of The Employee: The most important topic in business. https://joshbersin.com/2021/05/voice-of-the-employee-the-most-important-topic-in-business/

8. Ibid.

9. Sideways. (n.d.). The Top 50 Listening leaders. https://ideas.sideways6.com/article/the-top-50-listening-leaders

Chapter Fourteen

1. Zenger Folkman. (2019). How Developing a Coaching Culture Pays Off. https://zengerfolkman.com/leadership-studies/how-developing-a-coaching-culture-pays-off/

2. Lill, D. (2021, November 24). Six Benefits of Coaching In the Workplace.

Talk Business. https://www.talk-business.co.uk/2021/11/24/6-benefits-of-coaching-in-the-workplace/

Chapter Fifteen

3. Pendell, R. (2017, December 4). Tomorrow Half Your Company Is Quitting (So Win Them Back). *Gallup*. https://www.gallup.com/workplace/236216/tomorrow-half-company-quitting-win-back.aspx

4. Robbins, M. (2019, November 12). Why Employees Need Both Recognition And Appreciation. *Harvard Business Review*. https://hbr.org/2019/11/why-employees-need-both-recognition-and-appreciation

5. Daunt, V. & Menzies V. (n.d.). Recognition programmes. Are they important? *Deloitte*. https://www2.deloitte.com/ie/en/pages/deloitte-private/articles/recognition-programmes.html

6. Gibson, K.R., O'Leary, K., & Weintraub, J.R. (2020, January 23). The Little Things That Make Employees Feel Appreciated. *Harvard Business Review*. https://hbr.org/2020/01/the-little-things-that-make-employees-feel-appreciated

7. Deloitte Greenhouse. (2019, June). The Practical Magic of 'Thank You': How your people want to be recognized, for what, and by whom. *Deloitte*. https://www2.deloitte.com/content/dam/Deloitte/us/Documents/about-deloitte/us-about-deloitte-the-practical-magic-of-thank-you-june-2019.pdf

Chapter Sixteen

8. Williams, B. (2021, July 19). What percentage of Gym Memberships Go Unused? *Exercise.com*. https://www.exercise.com/learn/unused-gym-memberships-percentage/

9. De Pree, M. (2004). *Leadership Is An Art*. Currency.

10. Holiday, R. (2020, April 21). We Are What We Repeatedly Do. https://dailystoic.com/we-are-what-we-repeatedly-do/

Chapter Seventeen

11. Qualtrics XM. (n.d.). What is a Good Net Promoter Score. *Qualtrics XM*. https://www.qualtrics.com/experience-management/customer/good-net-promoter-score/

Chapter Eighteen

12. Gruenert, S & Whitaker, T. (2019). *Committing to the culture: how leaders can create and sustain positive schools.* ASCD.

13. Center for Creative Leadership. https://www.ccl.org/

14. Davey, L. (2015). Deliver Feedback That Sticks. *Harvard Business Review*. https://hbr.org/2015/08/deliver-feedback-that-sticks

Chapter Nineteen

1. Mazzetti, M. (2023, January 4). Understanding Customer Expectations: Management Tips and Examples. *Zendesk*. https://www.zendesk.com/au/blog/customer-expectations-meet-rising-demands/

2. Ibid.

Chapter Twenty

3. Ross, D.B., Exposito, J.A. & Kennedy, T. (2017). Stress and Its Relationship to Leadership and a Healthy Workplace Culture. *IGI Global*. https://www.igi-global.com/chapter/stress-and-its-relationship-to-leadership-and-a-healthy-workplace-culture/159290

4. Seligman, M. (2011). *Learned Optimism.* William Heinemann.

5. Brown, J. & Wong, J. (2017, June 6). How Gratitude Changes You and Your Brain. *Greater Good Magazine.* https://greatergood.berkeley.edu/article/item/how_gratitude_changes_you_and_your_brain

6. Robbins, T. *Unleash the Power Within.* https://www.upwnow.com/march-2023#section--61094

7. Covey, S.R. (1989). *The 7 Habits of Highly Effective People: Powerful lessons in personal change.* Simon and Schuster.

8. Mejia, Z. (2022, October 20). 10 Science-Backed Benefits of Meditation. *Forbes Health*. https://www.forbes.com/health/mind/benefits-of-meditation/

9. Pir, S. (2020, September 27). Caring In The Workplace: Why allyship matters more than ever now. *Forbes*. https://www.forbes.com/sites/sesilpir/2020/09/27/caring-in-the-workplace-why-allyship-matters-more-than-ever-now/

10. PricewaterhouseCoopers. (2021). Upskilling Hopes and Fears 2021. *PwC*. https://www.pwc.com/gx/en/issues/upskilling/hopes-and-fears.html

11. Sons, T. (2022, November 4). How Corporate Social Responsibility Appeals to Your Customers. *Forbes*. https://www.forbes.com/sites/forbesbusinesscouncil/2022/11/04/how-corporate-social-responsibility-appeals-to-your-customers/?sh=189ea41c3610

12. Calkins, T. (2021, January 20). COVID Has Forever Changed the Customer Experience. *Kellogg Insight*. https://insight.kellogg.northwestern.edu/article/customer-experience-covid-innovation

13. Stories from Hilton. (2021, April 20). Hilton Releases 2020 ESG Report, Reinforcing Commitment to Positive Global Impact. *Hilton*. https://stories.hilton.com/releases/hilton-report-highlights-positive-global-impact

14. Walters, D., Herbst, D., & Grossman Kantor, W. (2021, September 01). PEOPLE's 100 Companies That Care: Meet the Employers Putting Their Communities First. *People*. https://people.com/human-interest/people-100-companies-that-care-2021/

15. Geenleaf, R. (2012). *The Institution as Servant*. The Greenleaf Center for Servant Leadership.

Your Leadership Legacy

1. Mackey, J. & Sisodia, R. (2014). *Conscious Capitalism: Liberating the heroic spirit of business*. Harvard Business Review Press.

2. De Pree, M. (1990). *Leadership is an Art*. Dell Books.

www.ingramcontent.com/pod-product-compliance
Lightning Source LLC
Chambersburg PA
CBHW042119190326
41519CB00031B/7554